LIES MY TEACHER TOLD ME

YOUNG READERS' EDITION

LIES MY TEACHER TOLD ME

YOUNG READERS' EDITION

*Everything American History
Textbooks Get Wrong*

JAMES W. LOEWEN

Adapted by Rebecca Stefoff

THE
NEW
PRESS

NEW YORK
LONDON

Requests for permission to reproduce selections from this book should be made through our website: https://thenewpress.com/contact.

ILLUSTRATION AND TEXT CREDITS
5, Library of Congress; 8, Committee on Public Information; 12, Smithsonian American Art Museum, Transfer from the U.S. Capitol.; 22, Werner Forman Archive/Bridgeman Images; 33 and 34, Library of Congress; 35, Wikimedia Commons; 39, U.S. Capitol; 51, Granger Historical Picture Archive; 55, National Park Service Archaeology Program; 56, Library of Congress; 58, Wikimedia Commons; 63, Library of Congress; 64, Metropolitan Museum of Art; 66, Wikimedia Commons; 69, U.S. Capitol; 77 and 79, Library of Congress; 81, Wikimedia Commons/Smithsonian Institution; 83, U.S. Department of State; 84, U.S. National Library of Medicine; 88, New York Public Library, Digital Collections; 90, D.W. Meinig/Yale University Press; 95, Library of Congress; 97, Amway Environmental Foundation; 113, *Harper's Weekly*/Online Books Page at University of Pennsylvania; 115, Samee Siddiqui; 116 and 117, Library of Congress; 119, *Harper's Weekly*/Online Books Page at University of Pennsylvania; 130, Wikimedia Commons; 141, Naval History and Heritage Command Collection; 144, 145, and 146, Library of Congress; 152, Andrea Ades Vasquez, American Social History Project; 160 ("What Did You Learn in School Today?" by Tom Paxton), © 1962, 1990 Cherry Lane Music Publ. Co., all rights reserved, used by permission; 163, Bettmann/Corbis; 168, Wikimedia Commons; 174, Newseum/Ted Polumbaum Collection; 181, Eddie Adams/Associated Press; 183, Ronald L. Haeberle/LIFE Image Collection/Getty; 184, Hugh Van Es/UPI/Newscom; 185, Universal History archive/UIG via Getty Images; 197 and 207, Library of Congress; 209, Boy Scouts of America; 218, Christopher Michel; 219, James Cridland; 221, Library of Congress; 223, The Norman Rockwell Agency; 231, Grant Wood/Amon Carter Museum of American Art; 234, Wikimedia Commons; 235, Fibonacci Blue; 243, National Park Service; Ansel Adams, Library of Congress Prints and Photographs Division

Published in the United States by The New Press, New York, 2019
Distributed by Two Rivers Distribution

ISBN 978-1-62097-469-8 (hc)
ISBN 978-1-62097-485-8 (ebook)
CIP data is available

The New Press publishes books that promote and enrich public discussion and understanding of the issues vital to our democracy and to a more equitable world. These books are made possible by the enthusiasm of our readers; the support of a committed group of donors, large and small; the collaboration of our many partners in the independent media and the not-for-profit sector; booksellers, who often hand-sell New Press books; librarians; and above all by our authors.

www.thenewpress.com

Book design and composition by Lovedog Studio
This book was set in Fair ield Light
Printed in the United States of America

18 17 16 15 14 13 12 11 10 9

*Dedicated to all American history teachers
who teach against their textbooks*

(and their ranks keep growing)

Contents

WHY I WROTE THIS BOOK—AND OTHER QUESTIONS ANSWERED

If you truly want students to take an interest in American history, then stop lying to them.

—A HIGH-SCHOOL STUDENT'S LETTER TO THE *SAN FRANCISCO EXAMINER*

READERS OFTEN SKIP THE "INTRODUCTION" OR "Foreword" at the beginning of books. They want to get to the book itself. When a reader *does* stick around for an author's opening pages, those pages might say more than the reader wants to know about how the book came to be written.

So here is something different. I am going to answer six key questions about *Lies My Teacher Told Me.* If you have questions about this book, I hope you'll find the answers here.

Q. What is Lies about?

Lies My Teacher Told Me is about two things. One is American history. The other is the way young people are taught American history.

I wrote *Lies My Teacher Told Me* because I believed that although Americans take great interest in their past, they were bored by the history courses they took in school. American history is full of fantastic, important stories. When told right, these stories have the power to hold audiences spellbound—including audiences of young people. Not only do these stories tell us what America has been about, they are still shaping our lives today. Americans of all ages need and want to know about our national past.

Yet too often high-school students hate history. If they can avoid it, they do, even though most students get higher grades in history than in math, science, or English. When students list their favorite subjects, history is always at the bottom of the list, not in every school, but nationally.

Something has gone very wrong. As a college professor of sociology, my specialty was the study of social structure—how social institutions, such as education, kept races and social classes unequal. I was often shocked by how little students knew about U.S. history after studying it in high school, and how misinformed they were about what they did know. This wasn't the students' fault. They weren't stupid. I decided to investigate the textbooks that teachers were using for American history classes, and the overall way we teach history to young people.

For the first edition of *Lies*, which came out in 1995, I reviewed a dozen thick textbooks. For the second edition, which came out in 2007, I reviewed half a dozen new, even thicker ones. I looked at them in light of what historians, social scientists, journalists, and other professionals know about various topics in American history, from the arrival of the first people to the terrorist attacks of 9/11/2001. I reported the discouraging results of my investigation in *Lies My Teacher Told Me*.

One of my goals was to show how our textbooks get things wrong, and to suggest how they could do better. But mostly I wanted to open people's eyes to some of the richness and complications of American history—and show them what a weak, watered-down, colorless version of it they were fed in school. And people got the message, as you'll see two questions down.

Lies is not a complete history of the United States. I did not have time or space to cover many important subjects, such as the histories of women, immigrants, or the labor movement in America. But *Lies* will shine a light on some parts of our history you probably haven't seen before. You might not even have suspected they were there.

Q. Does Lies *attack teachers?*

Sadly, a few teachers rejected *Lies My Teacher Told Me* without reading it. The title made them think that I am a teacher basher. Yet the book never bashes teachers.

I have great respect for teachers, from kindergarten through high school. Many work in crowded classrooms for eight hours a day—and on top of that, they have to read and comment on homework, prepare and grade exams, and develop lesson plans. When are they supposed to research what they teach in American history? During their unpaid weekends and summers?

Lies did reach and move many teachers. This is important, because one teacher can reach a hundred students, and another hundred the next year. Many history teachers are serious about their subject. They study it themselves, they encourage students to research subjects that interest them, and they promote discussion in the classroom. But too many teachers simply rely on the textbooks (which they don't choose). As I discovered, textbooks have been doing a pretty bad job. If teachers have better tools, and if they go beyond textbooks, they will be better teachers.

Q. How did people react to Lies *after it came out?*

From the first day, readers made *Lies My Teacher Told Me* a success. As far as I can tell, it is the bestselling book by a living sociologist. A lot of people have written to tell me what they thought of it. A woman from Utah said, "For all these years (I am 49), I have had the opinion that I don't like history. . . . Thank you for your work. You have changed my life."

Lies inspired some readers to go back to school or change careers. "Words cannot describe how much your book has changed me," wrote a woman from New York City. "It's like seeing everything through new eyes. The eyes of truth as I like to call it." A lot of adults turned to *Lies* because they sensed that something had been wrong with their boring high-school history courses. They wrote to tell me that they had read the book twice, or bought copies of it to give as gifts.

Not every reader loved the book. "What a piece of racist trash," said an anonymous postcard from El Paso, Texas. "Take your sour mind to Africa where you can adjust *that* history." That was a very white response. The response from Native Americans and African Americans—and from many other white readers—was positive. A professor at Hampton University said, "My students, who are all African Americans, were immensely enthused and energized by your book."

Even young students are energized when they learn firsthand about history outside the covers of their textbooks. A fifth-grade teacher in rural Virginia wrote to tell me that at the start of each year, his students say they hate history. Two weeks later, all or most of them love it. What makes the difference? He gets his students involved with history beyond the textbook. They read primary sources, such as newspaper articles from the time period they are studying. They check out books by scholars of history. They "get away from the sanitized vanilla yogurt in the textbooks," the teacher said, "and shoot for a five-alarm chili type of history." But when the next teacher steers these kids back to the textbook, they raise questions and objections. "They become politically active within the middle school," their fifth-grade teacher reported. "They look like they will become good citizens."

Q. What did students say about Lies?

Students took matters into their own hands after the first edition of *Lies* came out in 1995. I heard from some of them. A fourteen-year-old in South Dakota wrote to tell me what she thought of *Lies My Teacher Told Me* and another of my books, *Lies Across America*. "These are EXCELLENT books," she said. "After reading them, I spread them around the school to different teachers. All were shocked and, due to this, are changing their teaching methods."

A high-school student wrote that he and his friends had "read your book *Lies My Teacher Told Me* and it has opened our eyes to the true history behind our country, positive and negative." He added that he couldn't wait to use the book as a reference in the American history class he would take in the next semester. A girl in North Carolina did exactly that. Her father wrote to me, "My daughter uses *Lies My Teacher Told Me* as a guerrilla text in her grade eleven Advanced Placement U.S. History and loves it—although the teacher isn't always as pleased."

One of my favorite emails came from a young man who said, "Dear Mr. Loewen, I really like your book *Lies My Teacher Told Me*. I use it to heckle my history teacher from the back of the room." I also heard from a few teachers who told me that my book, in the hands of their students, had made their lives miserable until they got their own copies, which shook them out of their textbook rut. These stories showed how the teaching of history can change from the bottom up. I hope this new edition makes it easier for you to bother *your* teachers with *Lies*.

Q. Why did you create this special version of the book for kids?

Young people have been reading the original *Lies* for years, it's true. But even some college students have complained that some words and sentences are too long. This version is meant to make it easier than ever for people of any age to read it and get a new view of American history.

Almost everything in this book comes from the 2007 edition of *Lies My Teacher Told Me*, with a few key facts and figures updated to 2019. The writing style has been made more kid friendly, and I've added some background information here and there to explain things that younger readers might not know. Just as in the original, all the sources of my information are listed in the Notes at the end of the book.

The main difference between this book and the 2007 *Lies* is that this one is shorter. It's been streamlined a bit to focus more on our history, less on specific textbooks and the textbook industry. (But there's still plenty of criticism of textbooks.) If this book leaves you hungry for the full *Lies* experience, you can always go on to read the original!

Q. *Have history textbooks gotten any better since the latest version of* Lies My Teacher Told Me*?*

I don't know. I doubt it. But I haven't read new textbooks since I wrote the 2007 edition of *Lies*. For years I've been saying that I would never review a third batch. "Nothing could get me to read another dozen high-school history textbooks," I tell audiences. "They are just too boring." I certainly *hope* textbooks have improved since the mid-2000s. Why not get hold of the one used in your school and see how it compares with the ones I talk about in *Lies*? For everyone's sake, I hope you decide that it *is* better. If not, speak up when you know it's wrong or incomplete.

LIST OF
TEXTBOOKS
STUDIED

Does your textbook "descend" from one of these books? Even if it does not, I suspect it suffers from the same problems that these books display. See what you think!

America: Pathways to the Present. Andrew Cayton, Elisabeth Perry, Linda Reed, and Allan Winkler (Needham, MA: Pearson Prentice Hall, 2005).

The American Adventure. Social Science Staff of the Educational Research Council of America (Boston: Allyn and Bacon, 1975).

American Adventures. Ira Peck, Steven Jantzen, and Daniel Rosen (Austin, TX: Steck-Vaughn, 1987).

The Americans. Gerald A. Danzer et al. (Boston: McDougal Littell [Houghton Mifflin], 2007).

American History. John A. Garraty with Aaron Singer and Michael Gallagher (New York: Harcourt Brace Jovanovich, 1982).

The American Journey. Joyce Appleby, Alan Brinkley, and James McPherson (New York: Glencoe McGraw-Hill, 2000).

The American Pageant. Thomas A. Bailey and David M. Kennedy (Lexington, MA: D.C. Heath, 1991).

The American Pageant. David M. Kennedy, Lizabeth Cohen, and Thomas A. Bailey (Boston: Houghton Mifflin, 2006).

The American Tradition. Robert Green, Laura L. Becker, and Robert E. Coviello (Columbus, OH: Charles E. Merrill, 1984).

The American Way. Nancy Bauer (New York: Holt, Rinehart and Winston, 1979).

The Challenge of Freedom. Robert Sobel, Roger LaRaus, Linda Ann De Leon, and Harry P. Morris (Mission Hills, CA: Glencoe, 1990).

Discovering American History. Allan O. Kownslar and Donald B. Frizzle (New York: Holt, Rinehart and Winston, 1974).

A History of the United States. Daniel Boorstin and Brooks Mather Kelley (Needham, MA: Pearson Prentice Hall, 2005).

Holt American Nation. Paul Boyer (Austin, TX: Holt, Rinehart & Winston [Harcourt], 2003).

Land of Promise. Carol Berkin and Leonard Wood (Glenview, IL: Scott, Foresman, 1983).

Life and Liberty. Philip Roden, Robynn Greer, Bruce Kraig, and Betty Bivins (Glenview, IL: Scott, Foresman, 1984).

Triumph of the American Nation. Paul Lewis Todd and Merle Curti (Orlando, FL: Harcourt Brace Jovanovich, 1986).

The United States: A History of the Republic. James West Davidson and Mark H. Lytle (Englewood Cliffs, NJ: Prentice Hall, 1981).

Chapter 1

THE PROBLEM WITH MAKING HEROES

*What passes for identity in America is a series
of myths about one's heroic ancestors.*

—JAMES BALDWIN

THE TEACHING OF AMERICAN HISTORY STARTS WITH heroification. This is the process of turning people into heroes. It's how textbooks and other media take flesh-and-blood men and women and make them into perfect creatures without conflicts, pain, or problems. The problem is that people who have been heroified may also be without interest.

What happens to heroes in textbooks and classrooms? Two good examples from twentieth-century America are Helen Keller and President Woodrow Wilson. He was an important president who gets a lot of coverage in most textbooks. She was a "little person" who did not make laws, declare wars, or make a scientific discovery, but teachers love to talk about her and suggest that their students read books about her.

Students learn something about both Helen Keller and Woodrow Wilson. But as you'll see in this chapter, heroification has twisted their lives so much that we cannot think straight about them.

Helen Keller as a Hero

Helen Keller could neither see nor hear. A teacher named Anne Sullivan helped her overcome these physical handicaps. Dozens of books, movies, and videos for young people tell of this remarkable achievement. Generations of teachers have held Keller up as an inspiration to students.

I have asked hundreds of college students who Helen Keller was and what she did. Most of them remember that she was a blind and deaf girl who was befriended by a patient teacher and learned to read, write, and speak. Some college students remember small details of Keller's early life—such as that she lived in Alabama, or that she was wild and had no manners before Sullivan came along. A few know that Keller graduated from college. Some say that she "wrote" or "became a humanitarian," but they know no details.

Keller was born in 1880. She graduated from Radcliffe College in 1904 and died in 1968. Writers and filmmakers have told the inspiring story of her early years but mostly ignored her adult years. After struggling bravely to learn to speak, Keller has been silenced by history. Most versions of her life story leave out the lessons she asked us to learn from it.

The Rest of Helen Keller's Story

The truth is that Helen Keller was a radical, someone who wanted far-reaching changes in society. Her particular form of radicalism was socialism, a type of economy in which the government owns and controls most of a country's sources of goods and wealth.

Even before Keller graduated from college she had become a radical. She joined the Socialist Party of Massachusetts in 1909. She cheered the Russian Revolution of 1917, in which radicals overthrew and assassinated an emperor. The Russian revolutionaries adopted the political system called communism, in which all citizens are supposed to be equal and the state owns all property, resources, and land. Keller called the Russian Revolution "the coming dawn."

Keller's commitment to socialism came from her experience as a disabled person and her sympathy for others with handicaps. Through research she learned that blindness was not distributed randomly through society. It occurred most in the lower classes. Poor men were blinded by on-the-job accidents or lack of good medical care. Poor women who became prostitutes risked blindness from sexually transmitted diseases. Keller saw how social class controls people's opportunities in life—sometime, as she learned, it even determines whether they can see.

Many Americans scorned and feared socialism in Keller's time (and afterward). Becoming a socialist turned her from one of the most famous women on the planet to one of the most notorious. Newspapers that had praised her accomplishments now insulted her intelligence. Yet she never changed her belief that our society needed radical change.

Having fought so hard to speak, Keller helped create the American Civil Liberties Union (ACLU) to fight for the free speech of others. In addition to raising funds for the American Foundation for the Blind, she supported the National Association for the Advancement of Colored People (NAACP)—a radical act for a white person from Alabama in the 1920s. Near the end of her life, she wrote to Elizabeth Gurley Flynn, leader of the American Communist Party. Flynn had been jailed as part of the U.S. government's attack on communists. Keller told her, "May the sense of serving mankind bring strength and peace into your brave heart!"

Not everyone will agree with Helen Keller's ideas and beliefs. Today her praise of Russia seems at best poorly informed. Some may even think it was treasonous. But few Americans even know she was a radical, because our schools and mass media have left it completely out of her story.

A President Against Democracy

What young people do not learn about Woodrow Wilson is even more remarkable than what they do not learn about Helen Keller.

Wilson was president from 1913 to 1921. When I ask my college students what they remember about him, they tell me that he led our country reluctantly into World War I. This conflict lasted from 1914 to 1918. It pitted France, the United Kingdom, and Russia (the Allies) against Germany and Austria-Hungary (the Central Powers). As the war went on, Turkey and Bulgaria joined the Central Powers. Italy and Japan joined the Allies. Eventually, so did the United States, under Wilson. The other

Women protestors demanding suffrage, or the right to vote. Wilson had suffragists like these arrested; his wife hated them. Yet their protests and arrests led to public pressure that made Wilson fear it would hurt him politically to keep opposing women's suffrage. In 1920, near the end of his presidency, the Nineteenth Amendment to the U.S. Constitution gave American women the right to vote.

thing my students recall about Wilson is that after the Allies won the war, he led the movement to create the League of Nations, an early version of the United Nations.

Most Americans don't know that some of Wilson's policies went against the principles of democracy, which call for a country to be governed by its citizens or the representatives they elect. But although democratic peoples make their own decisions, one of Wilson's policies was to use military force to interfere in foreign countries.

Wilson treated independent Latin American nations as though they were U.S. colonies. During his presidency, the

United States sent troops to Latin America more often than at any other time in our history. We landed troops in Mexico in 1914, Haiti in 1915, the Dominican Republic in 1916, Mexico again in 1917 (and nine more times while Wilson was president), Cuba in 1917, and Panama in 1918. Throughout his presidency, Wilson kept U.S. troops in Nicaragua. He used them to pick that country's president and force a treaty that favored the United States.

Wilson also interfered in Russia. He sent money and troops to help overthrow the communist revolutionaries. U.S. troops did not leave Russia until 1920. Only two of the eighteen history textbooks I surveyed mentioned this war. Yet Wilson's actions fueled Soviet hostility and mistrust toward the United States for decades afterward.

Textbooks do a better job of covering Wilson's invasions of Latin America. It is fascinating, though, to see the authors try to come up with reasons for these invasions—because an accurate account of them could not possibly make Wilson or the United States look good. Even in the 1910s, Wilson's actions in Latin America were unpopular in the United States. We now know that his interference in Latin American countries set the stage for dictators who later took control in those nations and made life worse for most people.

Many textbooks in my survey wriggled to get the hero off the hook. *Challenge of Freedom*, one of the older books, said, "President Wilson wanted the United States to build friendships with the countries of Latin America. However, he found this difficult." Several textbooks blamed the invasions on the countries that the United States invaded. *American Pageant*, one of the newer books, said, "Wilson reluctantly dispatched marines [to Haiti] to protect American lives and property." This is sheer invention. No evidence suggests that Wilson was at all reluctant to send troops to the Caribbean.

Every textbook did mention Wilson's 1914 invasion of Mexico, but each one suggested that it was somehow not Wilson's fault. *American Pageant* even said that "President Wilson stood firm against demands [from some Americans] to step in." But Wilson *did* order troops to Mexico, even before Congress gave him authority to do so. Historian Walter Karp has shown that the invasion of Mexico was Wilson's idea from the start. It upset Congress, the American people, and both sides in Mexico's civil war. Finally, under pressure from public opinion at home and around the world, Wilson ordered U.S. troops out of Mexico.

Wilson's presidential administration was the first to be obsessed with communism not just in the United States but in other countries. He said bluntly that to follow communism was "to be an apostle of the night, of chaos, of disorder." Wilson helped keep communist Russia out of the peace talks that followed World War I. After a communist rose to power in Hungary, Wilson helped cast him out of power.

Wilson claimed to believe in democracy and in self-determination, which is the right of a people or country to determine its own fate. But that belief never had a chance against his anticommunism. At the peace talks, a young Vietnamese communist named Ho Chi Minh appealed to Wilson for self-determination for Vietnam, which France controlled as a colony. Wilson refused to listen, and France kept its grip on much of Southeast Asia for decades to come.

Spies *and* Lies

German agents are everywhere, eager to gather scraps of news about our men, our ships, our munitions. It is still possible to get such information through to Germany, where thousands of these fragments—often individually harmless—are patiently pieced together into a whole which spells death to American soldiers and danger to American homes.

But while the enemy is most industrious in trying to collect information, and his systems elaborate, he is *not* superhuman—indeed he is often very stupid, and would fail to get what he wants were it not deliberately handed to him by the carelessness of loyal Americans.

Do not discuss in public, or with strangers, any news of troop and transport movements, or bits of gossip as to our military preparations, which come into your possession.

Do not permit your friends in service to tell you—or write you—"inside" facts about where they are, what they are doing and seeing.

Do not become a tool of the Hun by passing on the malicious, disheartening rumors which he so eagerly sows. Remember he asks no better service than to have you spread his lies of disasters to our soldiers and sailors, gross scandals in the Red Cross, cruelties, neglect and wholesale executions in our camps, drunkenness and vice in the Expeditionary Force, and other tales certain to disturb American patriots and to bring anxiety and grief to American parents.

And do not wait until you catch someone putting a bomb under a factory. Report the man who spreads pessimistic stories, divulges—or seeks—confidential military information, cries for peace, or belittles our efforts to win the war.

Send the names of such persons, even if they are in uniform, to the Department of Justice, Washington. Give all the details you can, with names of witnesses if possible—show the Hun that we can beat him at his own game of collecting scattered information and putting it to work. The fact that you made the report will not become public.

You are in contact with the enemy today, just as truly as if you faced him across No Man's Land. In your hands are two powerful weapons with which to meet him—discretion and vigilance. *Use them.*

COMMITTEE ON PUBLIC INFORMATION
8 JACKSON PLACE, WASHINGTON, D. C.

Contributed through Division of Advertising

United States Gov't Comm. on Public Information

Creel Committee Advertising in the "Saturday Evening Post"

Being antiwar was dangerous, once the United States entered World War I. People were invited to report to the Justice Department anyone who "cries for peace" or criticizes "our efforts to win the war." The Wilson administration's attacks on civil liberties such as free speech grew even stronger after the war.

Wilson and Racism

Wilson's interference in other countries was not his only anti-democratic policy. At home, he disgraced the presidency with his racism.

Before Wilson, presidents had regularly appointed African Americans to a few important government positions. Woodrow Wilson changed that—even though many African Americans had voted for him in 1912.

Wilson was a white supremacist, someone who believed that white people were superior to other races and should control the country. He told racist jokes in Cabinet meetings. His administration prepared a sweeping program to limit the civil rights of African Americans. When Congress refused to pass this program, Wilson used his power as chief executive to bring racial segregation into the federal government.

The navy was not segregated until Wilson limited African Americans to low-level roles such as dishwashers and waiters. He gave Southern whites federal jobs that African Americans had filled. His administration used the excuse of anticommunism to spy on and undermine black newspapers and organizations. The only time Wilson met with African American leaders in the White House was a disaster—he practically threw them out of his office.

Of the history textbooks I reviewed, eight never mentioned Wilson's racism. Only four accurately described his racial policies. Most of them gave Wilson's racism only a sentence or two. *Land of Promise*, way back in 1983, did the best job, calling out Wilson for his racism and his broken promises to black people.

Leaving out or excusing Wilson's racism goes beyond hiding

"Writing History with Lightning": A Landmark Racist Movie

White Americans burst out in violence toward African Americans during and after Woodrow Wilson's presidency. One reason was the racist example set by Wilson and his administration. Another reason was America's first epic movie.

In 1915 filmmaker D.W. Griffith made a movie called *The Clansman*, later changed to *The Birth of a Nation*. It was a tribute to the white terrorist organization called the Ku Klux Klan. The film celebrated the Klan for its role in putting down "black-dominated" state governments in the South after the end of the Civil War in 1865. In it, Griffith quoted from a history of the United States written by Wilson—one that is now notorious for its racist views. Wilson saw the film in a private screening at the White House. He said, "It is like writing history with lightning, and my only regret is that it is all so true." Griffith would use this quote to successfully defend his film against charges of racism from the NAACP.

This landmark American film was the best technical production of its time. It was probably also the most racist major movie of all time. And it led to action. Spurred by *The Birth of a Nation*, William Simmons of Georgia reestablished the Ku Klux Klan, a racist secret society that had flourished in the South after the Civil War. Racism seeping down from the White House encouraged this new Klan, which quickly became a national phenomenon. Klan rallies in the 1920s from Montpelier, Vermont, to Medford, Oregon, were the largest public gatherings in many towns' histories. During Wilson's second term, a wave of antiblack riots swept the country. In lynchings, or public murders, whites hanged, shot, and burned blacks as far north as Duluth, Minnesota.

Americans can learn from the Wilson era that there is a connection between a racist president and a racist response from the public. For this to happen, however, textbooks would have to show plainly not just Wilson's racism but also the link between hero and followers.

a character flaw. It is racist history. No African American could ever consider Woodrow Wilson a hero. Textbooks that heroify him are written from an antiblack point of view.

Protecting Wilson

Textbooks take pains to make it seem that Wilson did no wrong. They blame "Congress," not Wilson, for passing two laws that seriously attacked Americans' civil liberties: the Espionage Act of 1917 and the Sedition Act of 1918. In reality, Wilson tried to strengthen the Espionage Act and win broad censorship powers for the president. Textbook authors also suggest that the pressures of World War I are an excuse for Wilson's attack on civil liberties. Yet in 1920, with the war long over, Wilson refused to sign a bill doing away with the Espionage and Sedition Acts.

Wilson's second term saw witch hunts against communists and labor unions, the organizations formed to protect and advance workers' rights. Textbooks blame the fact that Wilson was ill, or claim that his attorney general was behind the witch hunts. No evidence supports these views. On the contrary, during Wilson's last days as president, a socialist and labor leader named Eugene V. Debs was serving time in prison for a speech he had given. Debs had said that economic interests had caused World War I, and that the Espionage Act was undemocratic. Wilson's attorney general asked him to pardon Debs. "Never!" Wilson replied. Debs stayed in prison until he was pardoned by the next president, Warren G. Harding.

Heroification of Wilson isn't limited to high-school history courses. His interference in other countries' affairs, his anti-communism, and his attacks on civil liberties fit our nation's

This marble statue of George Washington, now in the Smithsonian, was carved in 1840 and inspired by an ancient masterpiece. Textbooks might like to show every American hero this way: ten feet tall, blemish-free, with the body of a Greek god.

policies abroad and at home between the end of World War II and 1989. During this period—called the Cold War because of the hostility between the United States and the Soviet Union (a communist state established in Russia and neighboring countries)—textbooks, history museums, television documentaries, and political commentators spread the image of Wilson as "good," "idealistic," and "ahead of his time." Wilson became a social archetype, a figure that stands for certain values and emotions in a society, whether it is accurate or not: "He was good and so are we!" As you will see in many places in this book, social archetypes run all through our ideas about our history.

People who manage history museums know that visitors bring their social archetypes with them. Some museums design exhibits to show that the archetypes are not accurate. Textbooks, teachers, and moviemakers should also teach against inaccurate archetypes. In fact, Wilson's true accomplishments could stand on their own. He helped enact some laws that benefited many people, and his speeches for self-determination stirred the world, even if his actions did not live up to his words.

No Warts Wanted

Why do textbooks promote images of admirable figures that are wartless—lacking any flaws? Authors may leave out things that many Americans hate, such as socialism or racism, to make historical figures appeal to as many people as possible. Some authors may feel that showing anything bad about our leaders is unpatriotic. This view goes back a long time. In the early 1920s the American Legion called textbook authors "at fault" for telling readers about the flaws and weaknesses of the "prominent heroes and patriots of our Nation."

The example of Helen Keller takes us even further. Leaving out the last 64 years of her life paints an incomplete picture of who she was. We teach Keller as an ideal, not as a real person. We want our young people to be inspired to overcome obstacles, just as she was. Keller becomes "the girl who overcame"—but for what?

Keller herself did not want to be frozen in childhood. She was not the first deaf-blind girl, or even the first deaf-blind American, to learn to speak and write. But she made it clear that the meaning of her life lay in what she did *after* she overcame her disability. When she was nearing 50, Keller wrote:

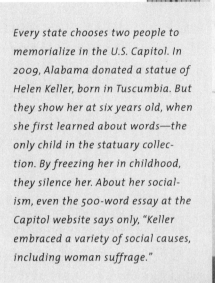

Every state chooses two people to memorialize in the U.S. Capitol. In 2009, Alabama donated a statue of Helen Keller, born in Tuscumbia. But they show her at six years old, when she first learned about words—the only child in the statuary collection. By freezing her in childhood, they silence her. About her socialism, even the 500-word essay at the Capitol website says only, "Keller embraced a variety of social causes, including woman suffrage."

I once believed that we were all masters of our fate— that we could mould our lives into any form we pleased. . . . I had overcome deafness and blindness sufficiently to be happy, and I supposed that anyone could come out victorious if he threw himself valiantly into life's struggle. But as I went more and more about the country, I learned that I had spoken with assurance on a subject I knew little about. I had forgotten that I owed my success partly to the advantages of my birth and environment. . . . Now, however, I learned that the power to rise in the world is not within the reach of everyone.

Textbooks don't usually touch this part of Keller's story because it raises the thorny subject of social class. It brings up the idea that America *has* social classes, that opportunity might depend on social class, and that not everyone has the same "power to rise in the world." Textbook authors would much rather present Keller as a simple source of inspiration to the young. So they leave out her adult life. They make this passionate fighter for the poor into something she never was in life: boring.

There are other reasons why history textbooks present characters without warts. Authors and publishers of texts might fear that their textbooks will not be chosen for use in schools if they are too honest. They might want to avoid uncertainty or conflict in the classroom. They might feel a need to protect children from troublesome facts.

There is a general feeling that we should speak respectfully about the past. We seem to feel that a person like Helen Keller can be an inspiration only when she is not complicated or controversial. As Keller herself pointed out, "People do not like to think. If one thinks, one must reach conclusions. Conclusions are not always pleasant."

Does Hero Making Work?

Heroification can cripple students. By keeping them from seeing the complications of figures such as Helen Keller and Woodrow Wilson, it keeps their minds from growing. It passes on what might be called a Disney version of history—our leaders as heroic statesmen, not imperfect human beings.

This way of teaching also prevents young people from understanding cause and effect in history. For example, when students try to understand why the Central American nation of Nicaragua embraced a communist government in the 1980s, it would help them to know about our country's thirteen military interferences there. Textbooks should also show how history is affected by the power of ideas and individuals. Instead, they show it as inevitable, a "done deal."

Do young people who have studied history in high school regard Keller and Wilson as their heroes? I have asked hundreds of (mostly white) college students to tell me who their heroes are. Some chose "none." Others showed the American trait of sympathy for the underdog. They chose African Americans such as Martin Luther King Jr., Malcolm X, or Harriet Tubman. Or they chose men and women from other countries, such as Nelson Mandela or Mother Teresa. As a rule, they did not pick the "establishment" figures who are held up in history textbooks for them to admire, such as George Washington and Abraham Lincoln.

In one sense this is healthy. Students should question what they are told to believe. But like other peoples around the world, we Americans need heroes. Who our heroes are, and whether we learn about them in a way that makes them lifelike role models, could shape our actions in the world.

We turn now to our first hero, Christopher Columbus. The nineteenth-century American novelist Washington Irving once said, "Care should be taken" to keep "great names" from being too closely studied. Irving also wrote a three-volume biography of Columbus. It was published in 1828 and still influences what textbooks say about Columbus today. It is no surprise that heroification hides important parts of Columbus's life and of our history.

Chapter 2

WHAT DID COLUMBUS REALLY DO?

In fourteen hundred and ninety-two, Columbus sailed
    the ocean blue.
In fourteen hundred and ninety-three, Columbus stole
    all he could see.

—TRADITIONAL VERSE, UPDATED

AMERICAN TEXTBOOKS HAVE GENERALLY PRESENTED Christopher Columbus as America's discoverer and first great hero. Unfortunately, many of them have left out almost everything that is important to know about Columbus and the European exploration of the Americas. Instead, they fill pages with made-up details to tell a better story, one they think will make readers identify with Columbus.

The traditional textbook account of Columbus goes something like this:

Born in Genoa, Italy, of humble parents, Christopher Columbus became a skilled seafarer. He sailed the Atlantic Ocean as far as Iceland and West Africa. His experiences told him that the world must be round. This meant that the fabled riches of the East—spices, silk, and gold—could be reached by sailing west. This would replace the overland route through the Middle East, which the Turks had closed to Europeans.

Columbus asked many European monarchs to fund an expedition westward to Asia. King Ferdinand and Queen Isabella of Spain turned him down, but Columbus finally got his chance when the queen agreed to pay for a modest expedition.

Columbus outfitted three pitifully small ships: the Niña, *the* Pinta, *and the* Santa Maria. *The journey was difficult. The ships sailed west into the unknown Atlantic for two months. The crew almost mutinied and threatened to throw Columbus overboard. Finally they reached the West Indies on October 12, 1492.*

Although Columbus made three more voyages to the Americas, he never knew he had discovered a New World, not a new route to the Asian lands known as the Indies. He died ignored, disappointed, and penniless. Yet without his daring, American history would have been very different.

Almost everything in this traditional account is either untrue or cannot be proven. Newer textbooks do better than older ones in their treatment of Columbus and what happened after his voyages to the Americas. Still, they get things wrong. Even worse, they leave out much that could help students understand the background and meaning of Columbus's voyages.

Many textbooks fall short in four key areas. First is the voyages to the Americas before Columbus. Second is the social changes in Europe that led to Columbus's voyages—and to Europe's domination of the world for 500 years afterward. Third is the story of Columbus himself, and fourth is the question of what Columbus actually did with his "discovery."

Why the quote marks around *discovery*? Because words matter. How can someone "discover" what someone else already knows and owns? For the same reason, calling the Americas a New World is a problem, because people had lived in the Americas for thousands of years when Europeans arrived.

Textbook authors are struggling to move beyond Eurocentrism, or showing history from a limited, European point of view. They do not always succeed. One of the newer books I surveyed, *A History of the United States*, opened the first chapter with "The discovery of America was the world's greatest surprise." The authors meant Columbus's discovery. Five pages later, they try to take back the word, saying, "It was only for the people of Europe that America had to be 'discovered.' Millions of Native Americans were already here!"

Taking back words has little effect. The authors' whole approach is to show whites discovering nonwhites, rather than two groups meeting each other. They are so Eurocentric that they did not even include the people of Africa and Asia on the list of those who had yet to "discover" America.

The Last "Discovery" of the Americas

Textbooks' first mistake has usually been downplaying explorers before Columbus. People from other continents reached the Americas before 1492. If Columbus had never sailed, other Europeans would soon have made the voyage. In fact, Europeans may have been fishing off the coast of eastern Canada in the 1480s, and maybe much earlier.

The question of when and how the *first* people reached the Americas, and where they came from, is covered in chapter 4. But there is evidence of many expeditions that may have landed in the Americas after those first inhabitants arrived but before Columbus.

We owe that evidence to archaeologists, scientists who learn about long-past societies from the physical objects they leave behind. These researchers also find clues to the past in the relationships among languages and in the genetics, or inherited DNA patterns, of the modern descendants of earlier people.

Some archaeologists think that ancient Roman seafarers visited the Americas, because coins from the ancient Roman world keep turning up all over the Americas. Native Americans also crossed the Atlantic. Two of them were shipwrecked in Holland in 60 B.C. and became major curiosities in Europe.

Historians and archaeologists do not agree about these and other possible early voyages. Some of the evidence of them is not strong. Still, if textbooks allowed controversy, they could show students which claims rest on solid evidence and which are on softer ground. They could challenge students to examine the evidence and make their own decisions about what really happened. This would introduce young people to the materials that researchers use to study the past—oral history, written records, cultural similarities, language, genetics, and archaeology.

Unfortunately, textbooks seem to prefer certainty. In *After the Fact*, a book for college history students, James West Davidson and Mark H. Lytle make the point that history is not a set of facts but a series of arguments, issues, and controversies. But in their high-school history textbook, *The United States: A History of the Republic*, the same authors present history as answers, not questions.

People and cultures moved around the world long before Columbus's time. In a sense, Columbus's voyage was not the first but the last "discovery" of the Americas. What do we know about some of the earlier ones?

Voyagers Before Columbus

Seafarers from Asia may have made it to the Americas. For example, South America and the Asian islands of Indonesia are separated by the Pacific Ocean, but they have similar styles of blowguns and papermaking. Some researchers think this means the two regions may have had contact thousands of years ago. In the same way, Japan and Ecuador share similar pottery and fishing styles. Could Japanese sailors have crossed the Pacific before Europeans sailed into the Atlantic *or* the Pacific? If such voyages did occur, were they explorations? Or were they epics of survival, with boats blown off course to distant landfalls? We will likely never know, but young people could be invited to think about these and other questions.

The Phoenicians, a trading and seafaring people of the ancient Mediterranean world, may have voyaged to the Americas. It is possible that Phoenician ships, perhaps with West Africans aboard them, reached the Atlantic coast of Mexico around 750 B.C. Giant stone heads from that time, carved by the Native people of Mexico, stand along that coast. They look like realistic portraits of West Africans. The first white person to describe them wrote in 1862, "[T]here had doubtless been blacks in this region." Others, however, think the statues are of Native leaders.

Evidence for possible African and Phoenician contact with Mexico includes similarities in the design of looms for weaving

Nine-foot-tall rock heads face the sea in southeastern Mexico. They were carved by Native American people called the Olmec. An archaeologist who helped uncover the Olmec heads thought they looked African. Others have said they look like certain facial expressions of Native children in the region or even like sculptures in Southeast Asia. One theory is that they represent Native kings.

cloth. Arab documents written centuries later seem to support such voyages. Some scholars dismiss this evidence as weak—but students could be encouraged to investigate, if their textbooks mentioned the possibility.

Most textbooks in my survey did mention the well-documented expeditions of the daring Norse sailors sometimes called Vikings. From the northern European region of Scandinavia they voyaged across the North Atlantic in stages. After establishing colonies in the Faeroe Islands and Iceland, they reached Greenland. Their Greenland colony lasted 500 years, from 982 to around 1500. During that time the Greenlanders traded with Europe. They also sailed west to parts of North America. They visited Baffin Island, Labrador, and Newfoundland in what is now Canada. They may even have reached New England in what is now the United States.

The textbooks that mentioned the Vikings in North America tended to say that they had no lasting importance. "They merely touched the shore briefly, then sailed away," said one. But Vikings built a settlement in North America and lived in it for two years, until conflict with Native Americans caused them to give up. Three hundred and fifty years later, the Norse were still harvesting wood in Labrador for their Greenland colony.

The Norse discoveries remained known to Europeans for centuries. In Scandinavia they were never forgotten. If Columbus visited Iceland in 1477 as he claimed, surely he learned of Greenland—and maybe of North America.

Even if the Vikings' voyages to North America did little to change the fate of the world, should textbooks leave them out? Of course not! No, we include the Norse voyages to give a more complete picture of the past. For the same reason, we could include earlier voyages and let students weigh the evidence.

African or Irish?

Two other sets of voyagers might have reached the Americas before Columbus, from Ireland and West Africa. How do textbooks treat them?

First, the West Africans. When Columbus reached Haiti, he found that the native Arawak people had spear points made of a metal they called "guanine." The Arawaks said they got them from black traders who had come from the southeast. The metal was a combination of gold, silver, and copper. It was identical to material used by West Africans, who also called it "guanine."

Islamic historians recorded voyages into the Atlantic from West Africa starting in around 1311. A century later, Portugal began sending expeditions to the coast of West Africa. They learned from these contacts that African traders had been visiting what is now Brazil. In the modern era, corpses have been found in Brazil that date from before Columbus's voyage and contain traces of common African diseases. Other bits of evidence from both sides of the Atlantic also suggest that Africans may have crossed that ocean before Columbus.

The second set of voyages is supported by evidence only from Europe. Irish legends written in the ninth or tenth century tell of monks who visited the "promised land of the saints" during a seven-year voyage centuries earlier. The legends include fantastical details, such as holding Easter Mass on the back of a whale and visiting a "pillar of crystal" and an "island of fire." Yet we cannot dismiss these legends as pure fantasy. When the Norse first reached Iceland in the ninth century, they found Irish monks living there. The crystal and the fire could have been an iceberg and Iceland's volcanoes.

Five of the twelve textbooks in my original sample mentioned the possible Irish voyages. Not one mentioned the West African voyages. Why would some textbooks mention Irish voyagers while none mentions African ones? Could it be unwillingness to think that the first non-Native voyagers to reach the Americas were black, not white?

Not from Scratch

Textbooks admit that Columbus didn't start from scratch. Every account of the European discovery of the Americas begins with the voyages sent out between 1415 and 1460 by Prince Henry of Portugal. Often called Prince Henry the Navigator, he is credited with discovering the Atlantic island groups of Madeira and the Azores, and with sending ships down the west coast of Africa. One of Henry's expeditions, led by Bartolomeu Dias, is recognized in textbooks as the first to sail around the southern tip of Africa into the Indian Ocean.

The textbook authors do not seem to know that ancient Phoenicians and Egyptians reached Madeira and the Azores and sailed around Africa before 600 B.C. Prince Henry knew of these Phoenician voyages. They inspired him to send his own expeditions. But they clash with one of our social archetypes—the idea that modern technology is a European development. The Phoenicians' early feats of sailing do not support the story that white Europeans taught the rest of the world how to do things.

None of the textbooks in my survey gave the Muslims credit for saving the works and wisdom of ancient Greek writers, for adding ideas from China, India, and Africa, and for passing all of this knowledge along to Europe through Italy and Spain. Instead, they showed Henry inventing navigation. Several books told how "the Portuguese invented a new kind of sailing ship— the caravel." In fact, Henry's work was based mostly on shipbuilding ideas and methods known to the ancient Egyptians and Phoenicians. These methods were developed further in Arabia, China, and North Africa. Even the Portuguese word *caravel* was based on the Egyptian word *caravos*.

Cultures do not form and grow on their own. The spread of ideas may be the most important part of cultural development. Contact between cultures often triggers a flowering on both sides. Anthropologists, who study human behavior, societies, and cultures, use the term *syncretism* to describe what happens when ideas from two or more cultures combine to make something new.

Schoolchildren learn that Persian and Mediterranean civilizations flowered in the ancient world because they were located on trade routes where cultures met and interacted. The story of Prince Henry is a golden opportunity to apply this same idea to Europe—but textbooks ignore it. One of them, *The American Way*, even said that before Henry, "people didn't know how to build seagoing ships." By "people" the authors meant "Europeans." It was a textbook example of Eurocentrism.

The Path to World Domination

American history textbooks do mention that social changes in Europe led up to Columbus's first voyage in 1492. But none of those I examined gave an in-depth explanation of these changes. Here is the story they told, pieced together with quotes from different books:

> *"Life in Europe was slow-paced." "Curiosity about the rest of the world was at a low point."* Then, *"many changes took place in Europe during the 500 years before Columbus's discovery of the Americas in 1492." "People's horizons gradually widened, and they became more curious about the world beyond their own localities." "Europe was*

stirring with new ideas. Many Europeans were filled with burning curiosity. They were living in a period called the Renaissance." "The Renaissance encouraged people to regard themselves as individuals." "What started Europeans thinking new thoughts and dreaming new dreams? A series of wars called the Crusades were partly responsible." "The Crusaders acquired a taste for the exotic delights of Asia." "The desire for more trade quickly spread." "The old trade routes to Asia had always been very difficult."

The level of scholarship is discouragingly low. The authors don't seem to know that the Renaissance was syncretic, blending ideas from many cultures to form something new. Instead, they argue for Europe's greatness in terms of mental qualities, such as "Europeans grew more curious." This makes sociologists smile. We know that nobody measured the curiosity level in Spain in 1492, or can compare it to the curiosity level in, say, Norway or Iceland in 1000, when the Vikings were voyaging.

Most textbooks note the increase in trade and commerce in Europe. Some point out the rise of nation-states ruled by kings. Otherwise, they do a poor job of describing the changes that led to the age of exploration and conquest. Yet historians know that six important developments in Europe paved the way for Columbus's voyages and the five centuries of European domination that followed.

1. Advances in military technology. Around 1400, European rulers began ordering ever-bigger guns. They learned to mount them on ships. This arms race grew out of the endless wars among Europeans. Military advances also included archery, siege warfare, and drill, which means training soldiers to move in formations. Eventually, Europeans used their advanced weapons against other peoples. They (we) still do.

2. New forms of social technology. In the years before Columbus, Europe made wider use of new tools for managing information, money, and people. One tool was the printing press. Another was a new type of bookkeeping that was based on the decimal system, which Europeans picked up from Arab traders. A third tool was bureaucracy, a form of organization with a head (such as a king or an elected or appointed leader) who gives some power to others (usually appointed by the head) to carry out duties and policies. A bureaucracy may have many levels of power, from directors to the managers beneath them to the workers at the bottom. People today think bureaucracies are slow and inefficient, but they work better than many other ways of getting things done. At the time of Columbus's voyages, bureaucracy let rulers and merchants govern far-flung ventures efficiently.

3. Changing values. Piling up wealth and dominating people came to be seen as the way to be admired on earth and saved in the afterlife. As Columbus put it, "Gold is most excellent; gold constitutes treasure; and he who has it does all he wants in the world, and can even lift souls up to Paradise." Sources from Columbus's time are perfectly clear about his motives. Michele de Cuneo, who went to Haiti with Columbus in 1494, wrote, "After we had rested for several days in our settlement, it seemed to the Lord Admiral that it was time to put into execution his desire to search for gold, which was

the main reason he had started on so great a voyage full of so many dangers."

Columbus was no greedier than the Spanish, English, or French. But most textbooks downplay the pursuit of wealth as a reason for coming to the Americas. Even the Pilgrims left Europe partly to make money, but you would never know it from our textbooks.

4. The nature of European Christianity. Europeans believed in a religion that could and should be spread to other peoples and cultures, one that served as a reason for conquest. (Followers of Islam share this characteristic.) Typically, after "discovering" a new group of American Indians, the Spaniards would read aloud—in Spanish—a statement called the Requirement. Here is one version:

> *I implore you to recognize the Church as a lady and in the name of the Pope take the King as lord of this land and obey his [commands]. If you do not do it . . . I will enter powerfully against you all. I will make war everywhere and every way that I can. I will subject you to the yoke and obedience to the Church and to his majesty. I will take your women and children and make them slaves. . . . The deaths and injuries that you will receive from here on will be your own fault and not that of his majesty or of the gentlemen that accompany me.*

The audience for these speeches, of course, could not understand what was said or agree to it. So they became fair game for conquest.

5. Success in taking over islands. In the years before Columbus, European rulers successfully took over island societies in the Mediterranean and the eastern Atlantic. In Malta, Sardinia, the Canaries, and later Ireland, they saw that island conquest was a route to wealth.

6. Disease. Diseases unknown to the Americas, such as small-pox, cowpox, influenza, and bubonic plague, arose in the connected continents of Eurasia and Africa. As you'll see in chapter 3, these diseases played a big part in the European conquest of the Americas. (They also helped Europeans take over Hawaii and Australia.) Most textbooks now include disease when they talk about the arrival of Europeans in the Americas. They typically say little or nothing about the other five factors listed above.

Europeans on Top

High-school students don't usually think about the rise of Europe—and later North America—to world domination. It seems natural, not something that has to be explained. Deep down, our culture encourages us to imagine that we are richer and more powerful because we are smarter. (Who, exactly, is this "we"?)

No solid or reliable studies show Americans to be smarter than other people. But because textbooks don't identify the real causes of European domination, or encourage us to think about them, the notion that "we're smarter" festers as a possibility. So does the idea that "it's natural" for one group to dominate another. The way American history textbooks treat Columbus

Bad Meat or Bad History?

When talking about the European voyages of "discovery," some teachers still teach what I was told decades ago. Europeans needed the spices of "the Indies" to disguise the taste of bad meat, but the Muslim Turks had cut off the spice trade. This forced Europeans to find sea routes to Asia. Three books in my original sample repeated this story. It is a complete falsehood.

As early as 1915, historian A.H. Lybyer disproved the story. Turkey had nothing to do with the development of new sea routes from Europe to the Indies. The truth is that the Turks had every reason to keep the old trade route open, because they made money from it.

This particular error was again exposed in a 1957 book called *The Modern Researcher*, which has been used in many college history departments. Some textbook authors probably read *The Modern Researcher* during their own educations. If so, the information did not stick. Maybe blaming the Turks for keeping pepper and cinnamon from Europeans fits better with the Western idea that Muslims are likely to be unreasonable or nasty.

Not a single textbook I examined told that in 1507 the Portuguese fleet blocked the Red Sea and Persian Gulf. Portugal did this to *stop* trade between Europe and the Indies along the old route, because Portugal controlled the new sea route around Africa.

supports this tendency *not* to think about domination and how it comes about.

The traditional picture of Columbus landing on the American shore shows him dominating immediately. He's dressed like a king, and the Native Americans are nearly naked. In reality, he would have been very hot, dressed like that in the Bahamas. But the appearance of domination is based on fact, in a way: right off the boat, Columbus claimed everything he saw. When textbooks celebrate this or fail to question it, they suggest that taking the land and overpowering the people was unavoidable, maybe even "natural." This is a shame. Columbus's voyages could be a splendid opportunity to teach about the social changes in Europe that I described earlier in this chapter.

As official missions of a nation-state, Columbus's last three voyages are perfect examples of the new Europe. Columbus carefully documented the voyages, including descriptions of the native people as ripe for conquest. He had personal experience of the Atlantic islands recently taken over by Spain and Portugal. He also had experience with the slave trade in West Africa.

Columbus's purpose from the beginning was not exploration or even trade. It was conquest and riches, with religion as a cover. Merchants and rulers paid for the voyages, and the second voyage, in particular, was heavily armed. If textbooks included these facts, they might lead students to think intelligently about why the West still dominates the world today.

Building a Better Myth

Take a moment to look back at the traditional textbook story about Columbus that opens this chapter. How much of it is based on fact?

Many aspects of Columbus's life remain a mystery. He claimed to be from Genoa, Italy, and there is evidence that he was. There is also evidence that he wasn't. He did not seem able to write in Italian, even to people in Italy. Some historians think he was a converso—a Jew who had converted to Christianity—from Spain, a country that pressured its Jews to convert. There are other theories about his origins as well. Historians who have

WHO IS THIS MAN?

1492 ✕ 1992

AN ONGOING VOYAGE
Library of Congress Quincentenary Program

Why does this T-shirt show six different faces of Christopher Columbus? Because although many pictures of him exist, not one was made during his lifetime. We have no idea what Columbus really looked like—although most textbooks include a portrait of him.

spent years studying Columbus say that we cannot be sure of his class background, either.

We do not even know for certain where Columbus thought he was going. Some evidence says he was trying to reach Japan, India, or Indonesia. Other evidence suggests that he wanted to reach "new" lands in the West. One possibility is that he wanted to find new lands, but said his goal was India so that monarchs would back his venture.

Disagreements among textbooks seem pretty scary. What was the weather like during Columbus's first trip? *Land of Promise* said his ships were "storm-battered." *American Adventures* said they enjoyed "peaceful seas." (Columbus's journal says the weather was fine.) How long was the voyage? Two months,

C. Columbus solicits funds for a promising project. Spain, 1489.

Without project funding, the world might still be flat.

according to one textbook, but nearly a month according to another. (One month is correct.)

To build a better myth, American culture held on for a long time to the idea that Columbus boldly forged ahead while everyone else thought the world was flat. The truth is that in 1491 most people knew that the world is round. Sailors in particular can *see* the roundness of the earth as ships disappear over the horizon—first their hulls, then their masts and sails, and finally the flags or pennants on top. Fortunately, the flat-earth fable is

Columbus's coat of arms proves that he knew he had discovered a continent—even though some textbooks claim he died without realizing it. On his third voyage, Columbus passed the Orinoco River. He knew it was too big to come from a mere island, and he wrote, "I have come to believe that this is a mighty continent, which was hitherto unknown." He later added a continent to his coat of arms (lower left).

all but dead. Only one of the textbooks I examined for the first edition of this book still repeated it. That book later changed the "flat-earth" story to "superstitious sailors . . . fearful of sailing into the oceanic unknown."

Sadly, other errors in the traditional Columbus story remain uncorrected. Some versions contain details supported by no evidence at all.

To build a better myth, authors tell of Queen Isabella sending a messenger galloping after Columbus and pawning her jewels to pay for the expedition. This fable is meant to make the odds against Columbus seem even greater.

To build a better myth, textbooks describe Columbus's ships as tiny and awkward. By today's standards maybe so, but in their time they were well-suited to Columbus's purpose.

To build a better myth, some textbooks have blown the crew's complaints into a near mutiny. Traditional versions of the story make the sailors seem superstitious and cowardly, while Columbus appears brave, wise, and steadfast. But sources from Columbus's own time give different versions of the sailors' behavior and Columbus's reactions. It seems likely, as one biography of Columbus says, that "[t]hey were all getting on each other's nerves, as happens even nowadays."

To build a better myth, some textbooks have claimed that Columbus faked the entries in his ship's log to make the voyage seem shorter than it really was. *A History of the United States* says that this showed that "Columbus was a true leader" because he did not want his men to feel they had gone too far from home. This detail seems meant to make readers think that the people who run things are smart, while those at the bottom are stupid and anxious. But Columbus himself wrote in his journal that he had faked the log entries in order to keep his route secret.

To build a more moving myth, textbooks have Columbus come to a tragic end—poor, sick, and unaware of his great achievement. In reality, he died well-off and left money and a title to his heirs. His own journal shows clearly that he knew he had reached a "new" continent—"hitherto unknown," as he put it. Surely this and all the other changes and additions to the historical record are meant to make readers identify with Columbus.

Finally, many of the textbooks I examined did mention that after the first voyage, Columbus made three more trips to the

A Spaniard Switches Sides

Some Spaniards of Columbus's time, such as Bartolomé de Las Casas, stood against the cruelty that Columbus brought to Haiti. Las Casas began as an adventurer and became a plantation owner. Then he switched sides, freed his Native Americans, became a priest, and fought desperately for humane treatment of the Indians. Las Casas called the slave trade one of "the most unpardonable offenses ever committed against God and mankind." He helped get Spain to pass laws that protected some Indians. Textbooks that gave the full story of Las Casas would show students an idealist and activist they could admire.

Americas. But most of them did not find space to tell us how he treated the lands and people he "discovered."

Conquest and Enslavement

In his four voyages to the Americas, Christopher Columbus introduced two things that changed the modern world and revolutionized relations among races. One was the taking of land, wealth, and labor from Native American peoples. Coupled with disease, this nearly wiped out some of those peoples. The other was the transatlantic slave trade. This created a racial underclass in the Americas.

Most of the islands Columbus reached were inhabited by the Arawaks. Columbus's first impression of these Native Americans was positive. He wrote in his journal that they were "very handsome," with eyes "large and very beautiful." Seeing a few golden ornaments, Columbus "gathered from them by signs" that gold could be found on the other side of the island, which was probably one of the Bahamas. When he got there, he saw several peaceful villages and wrote these menacing words: "I could conquer the whole of them with 50 men and govern them as I pleased."

On that first voyage, Columbus kidnapped ten to 25 Arawaks and took them back to Spain, along with parrots and gold trinkets. Only seven or eight Arawaks survived the journey, but they caused a stir in the royal court. The Spanish monarchy promptly outfitted Columbus for a second voyage with seventeen ships, 1,200 to 1,500 men, cannons, crossbows, guns, mounted soldiers, and attack dogs. The purpose was conquest.

Columbus reached Haiti and demanded that the people turn over food, gold, cloth—anything the Spaniards wanted, including women. American Indians who committed even minor offenses had their noses or ears cut off to show what the Spaniards could do. Finally, the Natives had enough and tried to fight back with their only weapons, stones and pointed sticks. This gave Columbus an excuse to make war. Bartolomé de Las Casas described the force Columbus used to put down the rebellion:

> For this he chose 200 foot soldiers and 20 cavalry, with many crossbows and small cannon, lances, and swords, and a still more terrible weapon against the Indians, in addition to the horses: this was 20 hunting dogs, who were turned loose and immediately tore the Indians apart.

Naturally, the Spanish won. Then, because Columbus had not yet found much gold but needed to take *something* back to Spain, he held a great raid and took a thousand captives. Columbus was excited. "In the name of the Holy Trinity, we can

Columbus Landing in the Bahamas *(above)* is typical of the heroic treatment of Columbus in most textbooks. Created by John Vanderlyn in 1847, it is one of eight huge "historical" paintings in the U.S. Capitol. An alternative illustration might show the impact of Columbus and his followers on the Americas. For example, in around 1588 Theodor de Bry illustrated the "New World" in woodcuts, some of which show Native people suffering under the Spanish *(below)*. They were seen throughout Europe and helped give rise to the "Black Legend" of Spanish cruelty. Other nations used the Black Legend to criticize Spain's behavior in its colonies, mostly out of envy. But textbooks have usually shown the activities of Columbus and his men as glorious.

send from here all the slaves . . . which could be sold," he wrote to the Spanish king and queen.

Hispaniola, or "little Spain," the renamed colony in Haiti, became a nightmare. Spaniards hunted American Indians for sport and murdered them for dog food. The Natives had to provide the Spaniards with either gold or cotton. Those who met their quotas were given brass tokens to wear. The tokens were good for three months. Indians caught with out-of-date tokens had their hands cut off.

All of these gruesome details are available in letters from Columbus and members of his expedition and in the writing of Las Casas, the first great historian of the Americas. Most textbooks in my survey made little or no use of these sources. If they did use them, they chose passages that reveal nothing bad about Columbus.

The Spaniards' demands were impossible for the Indians to meet. So Columbus introduced the *encomienda* system, in which he "gave" whole Indian villages to Spanish colonists. Because this system of forced labor was not called slavery, it escaped the criticism that slavery received. The encomienda system later spread across Spain's new colonies in Mexico, Peru, and Florida.

Native Americans couldn't stand the cruelty. They committed suicide by the hundreds. Women refused to bear children or even killed their babies "so as not to leave them in such oppressive slavery," as a Spaniard wrote in 1517. To her credit, Queen Isabella was against outright enslavement. She even returned some American Indians to their homelands. But other nations rushed to copy Columbus. Portugal, England, and France shipped whole populations of Native Americans off in bondage.

Portraying Columbus and the "New World"

The combination of the slave trade and new European diseases destroyed American Indian populations. Whole regions of the Americas were emptied. The deaths of the Indians meant that enslaving Indians could not solve Europeans' demand for cheap labor. As a result, Europeans turned to large-scale slave traffic in the opposite direction, from Africa to the Americas. Columbus's son started this trade, on Haiti. Then, in 1519, Haiti became the site of the Americas' first large-scale slave revolt when blacks and Native Americans banded together. The Spanish did not bring the uprising under control until the 1530s.

Of the eighteen textbooks I examined, one new one, *The Americans*, revealed the conflict on Haiti. It quoted Las Casas, who wrote that the savage methods of the Spanish would end only "when there are no more land or people to subjugate and destroy in this part of the world." One of the older books, *The American Adventure*, associated Columbus with slavery. One old and one new one let it go with something like "Columbus proved to be a far better navigator than governor." The other books, old and new, mostly adore him.

Clearly, most of these textbooks were not about teaching the true history of Columbus. They seemed to be about building character. They treated Columbus as America's origin myth: He was good and so are we. Presidents still say these things: in October 2017, President Donald Trump said that Columbus "inspired countless others to pursue their dreams and their convictions."

Textbook authors who used Columbus to build character clearly had no interest in telling what he did with the Americas once he reached them. Yet that is half of the story, and perhaps the more important half.

The Clash of Cultures

Columbus's second expedition launched what journalist Kirk-patrick Sale has called "the clash of cultures that was to echo down five centuries." To understand either European or American history, it is necessary to know something about Columbus's harsh treatment of the Native Americans. His methods are a major part of his legacy. After all, they worked. They drove the American Indians into servitude or death.

The voyages of Columbus forever changed the Americas, but they brought almost as much change to Europe. Crops, animals, diseases, and ideas began to cross the Atlantic in both directions. In 1972, historian Alfred W. Crosby Jr. coined the term "Columbian exchange" for this vast and far-reaching process. One result was the rise of racial thinking. People in Europe before Columbus didn't think of themselves as "white"—they were Spanish, French, and so on. But once the transatlantic slave trade was under way, Europeans started to see themselves as having something in common, as opposed to Native Americans and Africans. They began to see "white" as a race and to see "race" as an important characteristic.

Politically, the Americas puzzled Europeans. Were the Native Americans examples of simpler, better societies from the dawn of time, or were they primitive savages? How could large, complex societies have arisen in Mexico and Peru without social organizations like Europe's? How could Native groups like the Iroquois Confederacy in New York or the Choctaws in Mississippi and Alabama govern large areas without much of a hierarchy—a system based on levels of power, status, and authority?

The Americas changed more than just the way Europeans thought. Almost half the major crops now grown throughout the world originally came from the Americas. Adding American corn to African diets caused the population of Africa to grow, boosting the slave trade to the Americas. Adding American potatoes and corn to European diets caused a population explosion in the sixteenth and seventeenth centuries, especially in northern Europe. This fueled the flow of Europeans to the Americas and Australia. It also shifted power northward within Europe, from Spain and Italy to England, France, Germany, and Russia.

Gold, silver, and other resources from the Americas enriched Europe. The precious metals replaced land as the basis for wealth and social status. Europe's new wealth undermined power in other parts of the world.

Not one textbook in my original sample talked about the global effects of the Columbian exchange. Since that time, the idea has seeped into American history textbooks. Most of them now credit American Indians with developing important crops. They also recognize that Europeans and Africans carried diseases, as well as animals such as pigs, horses, and cattle, to the Americas.

Yet the two-way flow of ideas still goes largely unnoticed. This robs young people of the chance to appreciate the role of Native American ideas in forming the modern world.

Two Views of Columbus

Some people have attacked the portrait of Columbus I present here as too negative. But I am not saying that we should start teaching American history by crying that Columbus was *bad* and so are we. History is more complicated than that.

Columbus's conquest of Haiti was an amazing feat of courage and imagination. It was also an outburst of bloody violence that set a pattern for enslavement and for genocide, the destruction of entire peoples. Columbus is important *because* he was both a heroic navigator and a great plunderer. If he were merely a navigator, he might be only a footnote in history textbooks, like the Vikings. Instead, he launched a great change in the world. After him, the world became divided between the exploiters and the exploited, the developed and the underdeveloped.

When history textbooks leave out the causes of Europe's world domination, they offer history designed to keep us from asking important questions. When they glorify Columbus, they nudge us toward identifying with an oppressor. Perhaps worst of all, when textbooks paint a simple portrait of a godly, heroic Columbus, they provide a feel-good history that bores everyone, especially kids.

Chapter 3

THE TRUTH ABOUT THE FIRST THANKSGIVING

How refreshing it would be to find a textbook that began on the West Coast before treating the traditional eastern colonies.

—HISTORIAN JAMES AXTELL

WHAT IF WE LEARNED AMERICAN HISTORY IN THE other direction? What if textbooks began on the West Coast and moved eastward?

The traditional story of Europeans in North America starts with the English colonies on the East Coast. It may begin in 1620, when the Pilgrims—who had left England in search of religious freedom—landed at Plymouth Rock. They founded what became the Massachusetts Bay Colony. Or maybe the story begins a little earlier, at Jamestown, Virginia. The first lasting English settlement in North America was planted there in 1607.

These versions of North American settlement don't just bypass the Native Americans who were here first, and who will be discussed in chapter 4. They also leave out the Spanish.

Many Americans do not know that one-third of the United States, from San Francisco to Florida, has been Spanish longer than it has been "American." Hispanic Americans lived there before the first English colonists left their homeland.

The first non-Native settlers in what is now the United States were actually Africans. They were enslaved people brought to South Carolina in 1526 by Spaniards who tried to settle there. Before the Spaniards gave up and left, the Africans rebelled, killed some of their masters, and escaped to join the Indians.

Less than 40 years later, Spain built a fort at St. Augustine, Florida. Farther west, Spanish Jews were living in New Mexico by the late 1500s. They had come there looking for a place to practice their faith. They were our first pilgrims.

Part of the problem is the word *settle*. "Settlers" were white, a student once pointed out to me. "Indians" didn't settle. And somehow the English came to be seen as settlers, but the Spanish are seen as intruders.

I've asked hundreds of college students, "When was the country we now know as the United States first settled?" Many of them answered "1620." If they had learned about the Spanish settlements, or about Jamestown, or about the Dutch who were living in New York State by 1614, they had forgotten.

No matter. The *myth* of American origins begins at Plymouth Rock in 1620. The textbooks I examined told the story in much the same way. This version is from *The American Tradition*:

> *After some exploring, the Pilgrims chose the land around Plymouth Harbor for their settlement. Unfortunately, they had arrived in December and were not prepared for the New England winter. However, they were aided by friendly Indians, who gave them food and showed them how to*

plant corn. When warm weather came, the colonists planted, fished, hunted, and prepared themselves for the next winter. After harvesting their first crop, they and their Indian friends celebrated the first Thanksgiving.

One Thanksgiving weekend I listened to a tour guide at the Statue of Liberty talking about how people came from Europe to "populate a wild East Coast." But as we are about to see, if Native Americans hadn't already settled in New England, the white newcomers would have had a much tougher time.

The Americas Before Europeans

The hotter parts of Europe, Asia, and Africa have been the breeding ground for most human diseases. That's because humans evolved in tropical Africa, and human diseases evolved alongside them. After mastering the use of fire, clothing, and shelter, humans moved into cooler climates. In northern Europe and Asia, cold was a problem for any disease-causing microbes that must spend part of their life cycle outside human hosts.

Some hardy microbes did survive the slow migration northward from humanity's origins in Africa. But even these were threatened when humans passed from Siberia, in the northeast corner of Asia, into Alaska, in the northwest corner of the Americas.

Whether they crossed to the Americas by boat or on foot, the first people to enter these continents were probably healthier than most humans have been before or since, because many diseases could not survive the frigid conditions so far north. Neither could some animals. People in the Americas had no cows, pigs, sheep, goats, horses, or chickens before Europeans arrived in the 1400s. Neither did they have diseases such as anthrax, cholera, smallpox, and tuberculosis, which pass back and forth between humans and livestock.

Social density also made Europe and Asia less healthy than the Americas. Many Europeans and Asians lived in cities and other densely populated regions where diseases could spread rapidly from host to host. Although there were some large Native American cities, and some areas of dense population, there were also many small-scale societies, such as the Paiute Indians of Nevada, who lived in isolated bands or family groups. Overall, Americans had fewer opportunities than Europeans and Asians to be exposed to diseases.

Native Americans also bathed regularly. Europeans bathed rarely because they thought it was unhealthy and immodest, but their poor hygiene actually contributed to poor health. Indians noticed that Europeans smelled bad. Squanto was a Native American who is remembered for his connection to the Pilgrims. He tried to get them to bathe, but failed.

For all these reasons, the people of North and South America were extremely healthy before Columbus. Their lack of diseases common to other continents, however, proved to be their downfall. Native Americans had not built up resistance to those diseases through evolution or childhood exposure. The microbes that Europeans and Africans brought with them doomed the American Indians.

The Great Plagues

Europe had seen terrible plagues, outbreaks of diseases that were often fatal. The most widespread outbreaks were pandemics, which attacked whole regions or continents.

One of Europe's worst pandemics took place a century and a half before Columbus, between 1348 and 1350. Bubonic plague, sometimes called the Black Death, killed up to 30% of the population of Europe. This disease and others swept through Europe in waves for centuries.

In 1617, three years before the Pilgrims landed at Plymouth, a pandemic swept through the Native Americans of New England. Some historians think that it was bubonic plague. Others suggest that it was smallpox, chickenpox, influenza, or a form of hepatitis. All were new to the Americas, so where did the disease come from?

For decades, fishermen from England and France had fished off the Massachusetts coast. They went ashore for water, firewood—and perhaps to capture a few American Indians to sell into slavery in Europe. They likely passed the disease to Natives they met.

New England's first great plague far outdid the Black Death. Within three years it wiped out 90 to 96% of the American Indians on the coast. An English eyewitness to the aftermath wrote that scarcely one in twenty was left alive—the highest death rate in human history. Whole Native societies were destroyed. That first plague was not the last. Smallpox and other diseases struck again and again. White colonists caught the diseases, too, but they usually recovered. Native Americans usually died.

Between the first edition of *Lies* and the second, the biggest change in textbooks' treatment of Native Americans was that authors started mentioning the European-carried diseases that killed vast numbers of Natives. Some of the newer textbooks even included drawings made by the Aztecs of Mexico that showed the horrors of smallpox. This is a step toward a more complete and accurate history of our county. But what effects did the plagues have?

Neither Europeans nor Natives understood that microbes are the true cause of disease. The Pilgrims saw the Indians' deaths as evidence that God was on their side. John Winthrop, governor of the Massachusetts Bay Colony, called the plague "miraculous" and wrote to a friend in England that God had "cleared our title to this place."

Many Native Americans believed that their god had abandoned them. Native religions could not explain what was happening. Native healers had no cure. Their medicines and herbs brought no relief. Like Europeans who had despaired during the Black Plague, many American Indians turned to alcohol, Christianity, or suicide.

Disease meant that for their first 50 years in New England, whites faced no real challenge from the drastically weakened Native Americans. A conflict did break out in 1631, but, as the minister Increase Mather wrote, "God ended the controversy by sending the small pox amongst the Indians. Whole towns of them were swept away, in some of them not so much as one Soul escaping the Destruction."

The same thing happened in other parts of the Americas. How did Hernán Cortés and his Spanish troops manage to capture the huge Aztec metropolis that is now Mexico City? The Natives defending the city fell to smallpox. When the Spaniards marched in, there were so many bodies that they had to walk

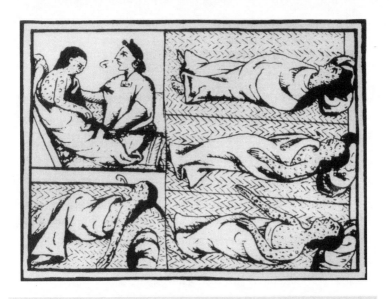

The Aztec people of central Mexico drew these images of sickness and death brought by the European disease smallpox. To the north, William Bradford of the Pilgrims described the horror of the smallpox epidemic around Plymouth: "[T]hey lie on their hard mats, the pox breaking and mattering and running into one another, their skin cleaving by reason thereof to the mats they lie on. When they turn them, a whole side will flay off at once as it were, and they will be all of a gore blood, most fearful to behold. And then . . . they die like rotten sheep."

on them. Most of the Spaniards were immune to the disease, a fact that helped crush the spirits of the Aztecs. It is still happening. Near the end of the twentieth century, miners and loggers carried European diseases to the isolated Yanomamo people of northern Brazil and southern Venezuela. The diseases killed a quarter of the Yanomamo in 1991 alone.

The early plagues are among the most important events in the history of America. By racing across the Americas, killing many of the Native people, the plagues made it much easier for Europeans to conquer and "settle" the continents. Europeans

How Many People?

The first epidemics made it hard to tell how many people lived in the Americas before Europeans arrived. Historians and anthropologists have hotly debated that question for years.

In 1840, George Catlin, a painter and traveler who spent much time with Native Americans, estimated that there were perhaps 14,000,000 people in the United States and Canada at the time of white contact. The Native population of his own time, Catlin thought, was about 2,000,000. By 1880, warfare and other pressures, along with disease, had caused Native numbers to drop to just 250,000.

In the twentieth century, estimates of the earlier Native American population dropped—maybe because of the power of the "virgin wilderness" social archetype of a thinly populated continent. A 1921 estimate said that just 1,000,000 people had lived in what is now the United States in 1492. Figures in that range were passed on until the 1960s and 1970s, when researchers began questioning them. Today, estimates based on careful research place the population of Canada and the United States before white contact at 10,000,000 to 20,000,000.

None of the original textbooks I examined told readers about the furious debate over Native populations in what is now the United States. They simply gave numbers—very different numbers. "As many as 10,000,000," said *American Adventures*. "[O]nly about 1,000,000," said *The American Tradition*. Five of them used that 1,000,000 figure, which had already become doubtful. Two said 10,000,000 to 12,000,000, which fits current scholarship. Two hedged their bets by saying 1,000,000 to 12,000,000, and three said nothing at all. None of the newer textbooks even raised the question.

The problem is not the number. It's the attitude. Presenting a controversy seems somehow radical to textbook authors. Controversy invites students to think for themselves—but textbook authors see their job as presenting "facts" for students to "learn." This keeps readers ignorant about how social sciences such as history use reasoning, arguments, and evidence.

never "settled" China, India, Japan, Indonesia, or much of Africa because too many people already lived there. The Europeans' military advantages might have let them dominate the Americas, as they eventually did other parts of the world. But it was the plagues that let Europeans "settle" them.

Because of the plagues, settlers such as the Pilgrims described their new home as a "virgin land," a wilderness only thinly inhabited by "primitive savages." Never mind that the land was not a virgin wilderness but a place that had been recently widowed by the deaths of its people. Yet the Pilgrims did know the truth. William Bradford, one of their leaders, told how the Dutch—who were rivals of the Plymouth colonists—went to an American Indian village to trade. He wrote, "[I]t pleased God to afflict these Indians with such a deadly sickness, that out of 1,000, over 950 of them died, and many of them lay rotting above ground for want of burial."

Virginia vs. Massachusetts

The Pilgrims' arrival in Massachusetts raises another historical controversy. The textbooks I examined said that the Pilgrims planned to go to Virginia, where there was already an English settlement at Jamestown. How did their ship, the *Mayflower*, end up in Massachusetts? Textbook authors duck the question.

"Violent storms blew their ship off course," said some. Others blamed "an error in navigation." Both explanations may be wrong. Some historians think the Dutch bribed the captain of the *Mayflower* to sail north to keep the Pilgrims away from the Dutch colony of New Amsterdam, in what is now New York. Others think that the Pilgrims went to Massachusetts on purpose.

Only about 35 of the 102 passengers on the *Mayflower* were Pilgrims coming to America partly for religious reasons. The rest were ordinary people seeking their fortunes in the tobacco plantations of the Virginia colony. Historian George Willison has argued that the Pilgrim leaders never planned to settle in Virginia, because they did not want to come under the control of the Anglican Church, England's official religion. They wanted a colony far from other English settlers. According to Willison, they planned to hijack the *Mayflower.*

The Pilgrims already knew what Massachusetts could offer, from the fine fishing to the "wonderful plague" that had cleared the land of its Native American inhabitants. Some historians think that Squanto, a Wampanoag from the village of Patuxet in Massachusetts, had described the area to a leader of the Plymouth Company in England, which was arranging the voyage of the *Mayflower.* The Plymouth Company may even have sent Squanto and an English sea captain named Thomas Dermer to Massachusetts to wait for the Pilgrims, although Dermer sailed away when the Pilgrims were late in arriving.

The Pilgrims may have had copies of maps that had recently been published, showing areas in New England—including Patuxet—that a French navigator named Samuel de Champlain had explored in 1605. John Smith of the Jamestown colony had also studied the region and named it "New England." Smith offered to guide the Pilgrim leaders. They decided he was too expensive and carried his guidebook instead.

For all these reasons, I believe that the Pilgrim leaders probably ended up in Massachusetts on purpose. But there is no firm evidence for any conclusion. In fact, the *Mayflower* may have had no specific destination. Students might be fascinated

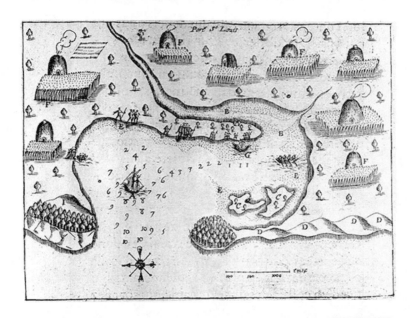

The Pilgrims' information about New England probably included maps made by French explorer Samuel de Champlain. He drew this chart of Patuxet (Plymouth) when it was still an Indian village, before the plague of 1617.

if textbook authors gave two or more of the possibilities, but each textbook picks just one and sticks to it as fact.

Only one textbook I examined raised the hijacking possibility. "The New England landing came as a rude surprise for the bedraggled and tired [non-Pilgrim] majority on board the *Mayflower*," said *Land of Promise*. "Rumors of mutiny spread quickly." *Land of Promise* then explained that to calm the unrest, the Pilgrim leaders did something "remarkable." They called for every adult man on the ship, no matter his social standing, to join in the democratic agreement that is known as the Mayflower Compact. This worked, and the majority of the passengers agreed to land where the Pilgrims wanted.

A heroic image of the Pilgrims landing at Plymouth highlights their bravery, strength, and chivalry. It does not hint at the disputes within the group.

This version of the story—a hijacking followed by a democratic agreement—shows the Mayflower Compact as a graceful solution to an awkward problem. But it makes the Pilgrims look somewhat dishonorable, which may be why only one textbook chose it. Storms and navigation errors are not actually very reasonable explanations, but they leave the Pilgrims looking pure of heart, which may be why most textbooks chose one of them.

Making America Exceptional

Whatever the Pilgrims' reason for creating the Mayflower Compact, it was a democratic basis for the Massachusetts colony.

Textbook authors lavish a lot of attention on the compact. It hardly deserves this attention, for it had little effect on the writers of our country's Constitution. But authors clearly want to package the Pilgrims as a moral band who laid the foundation for America's self-government.

This was embarrassingly obvious in *American History*, one of the books in my survey. It said, "So far as any record shows, this was the first time in human history that a group of people consciously created a government where none had existed before." The textbook took this idea from an 1802 speech by John Adams, a founder and early president of the United States. Both Adams and *American History* failed to note the Republic of Iceland, the Iroquois Confederacy, and countless other governments created before 1620.

In their treatment of the Pilgrims, textbooks introduce the social archetype of American exceptionalism. This is the notion that the United States is different from, and better than, all other nations on the planet. We're exceptionally nice, for one thing. As Woodrow Wilson put it, "We're the only idealistic nation in the world." And we're "the world's oldest republic," in the words of *The American Pageant*. Never mind that Iceland became a republic—a country governed by elected representatives, with some citizens' rights guaranteed by law—in 930 and Switzerland in around 1300.

America's outstanding qualities are clear from the "beginning" at Plymouth Rock, according to the textbooks. *A History of the United States* said that the Pilgrims "were equipped with just the right combination of hopes and fears, optimism and pessimism, self-confidence and humility to be successful settlers. And this was one of the most fortunate coincidences in our history." This happy picture of the Pilgrims left out the plague, the

Nationalism is part of the appeal of President Donald Trump, whose campaign sold hats (made in China) with his "Make America Great Again" slogan. In October 2018, Trump said at a rally, "You know what I am? I'm a nationalist."

possible hijacking, and the ways the settlers would soon interact with American Indians.

Textbooks highlight that happy picture by downplaying the Spanish settlements and Jamestown. This lets Plymouth Rock stand out as the archetype of America's birthplace. Textbooks could hardly celebrate Virginia as having moral origins, after all. The first history of Virginia that was written by a Virginian says that the colonists' main goal was to "fetch away the Treasure," not to "form any regular Colony."

Perhaps textbooks downplay Jamestown because the Virginians' relations with American Indians were unsavory. The colonists took Native prisoners and forced them to teach farming. In 1623 the colonists used chemical warfare. They poisoned a chief, his family and advisors, and 200 of his followers. The early Virginians also engaged in bickering, laziness, and even cannibalism. They spent their early days digging random holes in the ground looking for gold rather than planting crops. Soon they were starving. Some dug up rotting Native corpses to eat. Others rented themselves out as servants to Native families in order to survive. These were hardly the heroic founders that an exceptionally great nation needs.

Textbooks do cover the Virginia colony, and they at least mention the Spanish settlement, but they spend at least 50% more space on Massachusetts. For this reason—and also, of course, because of Thanksgiving—students are much more likely to remember the Pilgrims as the nation's founders. That's why almost all my students know the name of the Pilgrims' ship, but almost none remember the names of the three ships that brought colonists to Jamestown. (For the next time you're on *Jeopardy!*, those ships were *Susan Constant*, *Discovery*, and *Godspeed*.)

A Head Start for the Newcomers

Have you ever wondered why the names of so many towns in New England end with *field*? There's Springfield, Deerfield, Marshfield, and more. It's because throughout New England, colonists took Native American cornfields for their own first settlements. This spared them the backbreaking labor of clearing the land of trees and rocks. European invaders followed this pattern all through the Americas, pitching camp right in the middle of Native communities.

The Pilgrims ended up many miles from other European settlements, but they hardly "started from scratch" in a "wilderness," as textbooks would like us to think. Native Americans had repeatedly burned the underbrush throughout southern New England. The land was more like a park than a wild forest.

When it came to picking a spot for their settlement, the Pilgrims chose a place with a brook and beautifully cleared fields that had recently been planted with corn. It was a lovely site for a town. In fact, it *was* a town—or the remains of one. The Pilgrims settled in Squanto's village of Patuxet. The plague had killed most of the Wampanoags. "In this bay wherein we live," wrote one Plymouth colonist in 1622, "in former time hath lived about 2,000 Indians."

No sooner had they landed than the English helped themselves to what they found. A colonist's journal tells how sailors entered two American Indian houses, "found the people were gone," and "took some things." The same eyewitness wrote about finding "corn, two or three baskets full, and a bag of beans. . . . In all we had about ten bushels, which will be enough for seed. It was with God's help that we found this corn, for how else could we have done it, without meeting some Indians who might trouble us." From the start, the colonists thanked God, not the Natives who had grown and gathered the corn and beans.

The eyewitness continued:

The next morning we found a place like a grave. We decided to dig it up. We found first a mat, and under that a fine bow. . . . We also found bowls, trays, dishes, and things like that. We took several of the prettiest things to carry away with us, and covered the body up again.

A place "like" a grave!

According to historian Karen Kupperman, the Pilgrims continued to rob graves for years. But they got more help from a live Indian, Squanto. All my students have learned the Squanto legend. This version from *Land of Promise* is typical of what the textbooks say about him:

> *Squanto had learned their language, he explained, from English fishermen who ventured into the New England waters each summer. Squanto taught the Pilgrims how to plant corn, squash, and pumpkins. Would the small band of settlers have survived without Squanto's help? We cannot say. But by the fall of 1621, colonists and Indians could sit down to several days of feast and thanksgiving to God (later celebrated as the first Thanksgiving).*

Squanto was indeed vital to the survival of Plymouth in its first two years. He was the colonists' translator, go-between with Native leaders, and advisor. Like other Europeans in America, the Plymouth colonists had no idea what to eat or how to raise or find food. They had to be taught by American Indians. William Bradford of the Pilgrims called Squanto "a special instrument sent of God. . . . He directed [the colonists] how to set their corn, where to take fish, and to procure other commodities, and was also their pilot to bring them to unknown places for their profit."

Note that Bradford referred to "profit." The primary reason the *Mayflower* colonists made the trip was to make money. This was true of most of the Pilgrims as well as the non-Pilgrims. Yet the colonists had neither the skill nor the desire to go on their own to the "unknown places" Bradford mentioned. They turned to the Natives, who helped them set up fur-trading posts in Maine, Massachusetts, and Connecticut. Without the fur trade, Plymouth would never have paid for itself.

The Real Squanto

What do most textbooks leave out of Squanto's story? For one thing, they don't give the full account of how he learned English. According to Ferdinando Gorges, an organizer of the Plymouth Company, in around 1605 an English captain stole Squanto and four other Natives and took them to England. Squanto was still a boy. He then spent nine years in England. For three of them he worked for Gorges. Finally Gorges helped Squanto get back to Massachusetts.

Some historians do not think Squanto was one of the five American Indians stolen in 1605. All agree, though, that in 1614 an English slave raider seized Squanto and two dozen other Indians from the American coast and sold them into slavery in Spain. Squanto escaped and made his way to England. In 1619 he talked the English captain Thomas Dermer into taking him along on his next trip to Cape Cod.

Here Squanto's amazing adventure meets the appalling story of the plague. For Squanto walked to his home village of Patuxet, only to make the horrifying discovery that "he was the sole member of his village still alive. All the others had perished in the epidemic two years before." No wonder Squanto joined up with the Pilgrims.

Now *that* is a story worth telling! How do you think it compares with the lifeless account in *Land of Promise*?

Thanksgiving

All this brings us to Thanksgiving. Throughout the nation, every November, we carry out this ritual. Young children make colorful turkeys and black Pilgrim hats out of paper. Schools present Thanksgiving plays. Families gather to feast on foods that we connect with the Pilgrims' first thanksgiving: turkey, squash, and pumpkin pie.

The First Thanksgiving *is part of a series of historical paintings made around 1900 by J.L.G. Ferris. With gracious, generous Pilgrims feeding humble Native Americans, the painting sums up our distorted view of this moment in history.*

More than any other holiday, Thanksgiving celebrates our sense that we are a special nation that was destined for greatness. We have already seen how the early Pilgrim leaders thanked God for the plague that killed Native peoples. To them, this proved that God was on the Pilgrims' side. That's one of the social archetypes tied to Thanksgiving. Another is the carving of civilization out of wilderness through hard work and good Pilgrim character traits.

Our traditional image of the first Thanksgiving shows the feast set up in the woods. Around it sit Pilgrims in their starchy Sunday clothes, next to American Indian guests wearing almost nothing. As a holiday greeting card says, *"I is for the Indians we invited to share our food."* Yet that first feast was provided by the Indians, or with their help. The Pilgrims had never seen turkeys or squash or pumpkins before coming to North America.

Turkey and Thanksgiving were firmly linked in Americans' minds by 1864, when artist Winslow Homer created this image of Civil War soldiers with a turkey's "wishbone." The message is that they are wishing for an end to the war.

The true history of Thanksgiving reveals embarrassing facts. The Pilgrims did not start the tradition. For centuries Indians in eastern North America had held harvest celebrations in the autumn. Our modern celebrations date back only to 1863, in the middle of the Civil War. At a time when the Union needed all the patriotism it could get, Abraham Lincoln made Thanksgiving a national holiday. The Pilgrims had nothing to do with it. They weren't even associated with the holiday until the 1890s. In fact, they were not commonly known as "the Pilgrims" until the 1870s.

Our Thanksgiving ritual pushes Native Americans to the edges of history. It is ethnocentric, meaning that it gives central importance to one culture, and that culture is white and European. After all, if our culture has God on its side, why should we take other cultures seriously? When textbooks promote this ethnocentrism with their Pilgrim stories, they leave students less able to learn from and live with people from other cultures.

Sometimes, the price of ethnocentrism is censorship. In 1970, the Massachusetts Department of Commerce asked the Wampanoags for a speaker on the 350th anniversary of the Pilgrims' landing. The tribe chose Frank James, but first the European Americans in charge of the ceremony had to see his speech. Once they had seen it, they wouldn't let him give it. James had written:

> *Today is a time of celebrating for you . . . but it is not a time of celebrating for me. It is with heavy heart that I look back upon what happened to my People. . . . The Pilgrims had hardly explored the shores of Cape Cod four days before they had robbed the graves of my ancestors, and stolen their corn . . . and beans. . . . Massasoit, the great leader of the Wampanoag, knew these facts; yet he and his People welcomed and befriended the settlers . . . little knowing that . . . before 50 years were to pass, the Wampanoags . . . and other Indians living near the settlers would be killed by their guns or dead from diseases that we caught from them. . . . What has happened cannot be changed, but today we work toward a better America, a more Indian America where people and nature once again are important.*

The speech that James was prevented from giving was historical truth. Most of our textbooks also leave out truths such as grave robbing and Native enslavement. Our popular history of the Pilgrims has not been a process of gaining insight. It

Turkey and football have become even more symbolic of the modern American Thanksgiving than they were when this vintage card was new.

has been one of deliberate forgetting. Instead of important and uncomfortable truths, the textbooks I examined supply feel-good stories and unimportant details.

The Pilgrims were undeniably courageous to set forth in late fall to make their way on a new continent. And like the Indians, they suffered. In their first year, half of them died from diseases such as scurvy and pneumonia. It was not immoral of them to take over the empty village of Patuxet. They had not caused the plague.

In addition, relations between the Pilgrims and the Natives started reasonably well. The newcomers did eventually pay the Wampanoags for the corn they had taken. Unlike many other colonies, Plymouth usually paid the Indians for the land it took. Sometimes Europeans settled in Indian towns because the Native people had invited them, seeking their protection against another tribe or a rival European power. In short, U.S.

history is no more violent than the histories of many other countries—but neither is it less violent.

The way to correct feel-good history is not with feel-bad history. It is with honest history that includes both the good and the bad. If the story of the first Thanksgiving were correctly taught, it could help Americans grow more tolerant and thoughtful, rather than more ethnocentric.

Today the town of Plymouth, where the myth started, provides a model for this way of teaching history. When Frank James was prevented from giving his speech in 1970, Natives and their allies did not take it lying down. That year and in the years afterward, they organized a counterparade called "the National Day of Mourning." After years of conflict, Plymouth agreed to pay for both parades. It also paid for two new historical markers to tell the Wampanoags' side of the story. But as you will see in the next chapter, many truths about Native Americans remain untold.

Chapter 4

THROUGH
RED EYES

*There is not one Indian in the whole of this country
who does not cringe in anguish and frustration because
of those textbooks. There is not one Indian child who
has not come home in shame and tears.*

—Rupert Costo

AMERICAN INDIANS HAVE BEEN THE MOST LIED-ABOUT
group in our population. Textbooks have long been part of the
problem. They have presented Native Americans through white
eyes.

Textbooks have begun to treat Native peoples better in
recent years. In 1961, the bestselling textbook *Rise of the American Nation* had 269 illustrations. Ten of them featured Native
people, alone or with whites. Most of these illustrations were on
themes of primitive life and savage warfare.

Twenty-five years later, a new edition of the same book, now
called *Triumph of the American Nation*, had fifteen images of
Native Americans. Better yet, they no longer depicted them
as primitives. Instead, they showed people who struggled to
preserve their identities and their land. Among the Natives
pictured were Crispus Attucks, the first person killed in the
American Revolution, who was also part black; Sequoyah, the

A nearly naked American Indian shakes the hand of a thoroughly dressed William Penn in this sculpture in the U.S. Capitol. If this meeting took place in August, Penn would have been near death from heat exhaustion. If it took place in winter, the Natives would have been suffering from frostbite.

inventor of the Cherokee alphabet; and the Navajo code-talkers of World War II, who used their Native language to help the United States and its allies win the war.

By 2003 the book, now called *Holt American Nation*, had 43 pictures of American Indians. Some other textbooks published after 2000 also gave more attention to Native Americans.

But textbooks could still do better. Even *The Americans*, a textbook that stood out in my survey for its honest treatment of American Indian history, filled its first two pages with a painting called *Penn's Treaty with the Indians*. American artist

Benjamin West painted this work in 1771, almost a century after the agreement was made between William Penn, the founder of the Pennsylvania colony, and the Native Americans of the region. The artist didn't try to show reality. Instead, he showed a social archetype—the archetype of civilized Europeans and primitive Indians.

West's painting follows the custom of the times in the way it portrays the two groups. Whites are dressed in full European clothes, including hats, scarves, and coats. They are handing out trade goods to American Indians who are nearly naked. In reality, two groups of people would never dress so differently in the same place on the same day. If they did, one group would either melt or freeze!

Some textbooks no longer use racist or demeaning terms that were once common, such as *half-breed, massacre,* or *warwhoop.* But as we saw in the last chapter, even milder terms such as *settlers* for "whites" are slanted. Imagine that you are from, say, the African nation of Botswana. Now read this sentence from *The American Journey*: "In 1637 war broke out in Connecticut between the settlers and the Pequot people." But, you would think, surely the Pequots, who had lived in Connecticut for thousands of years, were the "settlers." The English newcomers had been there for three years at most. If you replace *settlers* with *whites* in the sentence, it is more accurate, but maybe a little uncomfortable. If you replaces *settlers* with *invaders*, it becomes even more accurate—and more uncomfortable.

Our journey into the history of American Indians' relations with European and African invaders cannot be a happy one. Native Americans are not props in a theme park of the past, where we go to see colorful cultures. If we look straight at

American Indian history through "red eyes," from a Native point of view, *we* may be the ones with red eyes, from tears of shame. This is our past, however, and we must recognize it.

The Question of When

Most of today's textbooks at least try to be accurate about American Indian cultures. Of the eighteen textbooks I surveyed, thirteen spent more than five pages on the Native societies of the Americas before contact with Europeans. However, textbook authors are not generally scholars in fields that study those societies, such as archaeology and anthropology. The authors pluck answers from books by scholars, but they do not include new discoveries or debates.

In reality, the field of precontact American Indian studies is alive with controversy. Take the question of when the ancestors of the Native Americans first arrived in the Americas. Nearly every year brings a new headline about possible remains of 40,000-year-old cooking fires found in Brazil, or new dates from an archaeological dig in Pennsylvania, or a claim that some object or idea might have reached the Americas from China or Africa.

"Possibly" does not fit textbook style. Textbook authors like to give definite answers. Various researchers have given estimates ranging from 12,000 to 72,000 years for the time that humans have been in the Americas. But only one of the textbooks I surveyed, *The American Adventure*, allowed for uncertainty. It presented competing claims for 12,000 years, 21,000 years, and 40,000 years. It also admitted, "This page may be out of date by the time it is read."

If we're not sure when, do we know *how* people got to the Americas? Every textbook said something about Beringia. This "land bridge" linked Siberia and Alaska during the last Ice Age. At that time, so much of the earth's water was frozen into vast ice sheets that ocean levels were much lower than they are today.

The usual explanation for the peopling of the Americas is that bands of hunters made their way across Beringia following the animals that were their prey. Then, said *A History of the United States*, "Without knowing it, they had discovered two large continents that were completely empty of people but were full of wild game. . . . In the thousands of years afterwards, many other groups followed. These small bands spread all across North and South America." Think about this language. What is a continent? It's a very large landmass. Australia qualifies; Greenland doesn't. I suggest that the first settlers in the Americas would have to have been very stupid indeed if they had discovered two very large landmasses without knowing it.

Another textbook, *American History*, also said that it took many thousands of years for humans to populate both continents. The authors have no idea whether this is true or not. They simply suppose that the first settlers were slow, and perhaps not very bright. In fact, many archaeologists think that people reached most parts of the Americas within a thousand years or so.

The second textbook went on to say, "None of the groups made much progress in developing simple machines or substituting mechanical or even animal power for their own muscle power." This was not the fault of the early Americans. No "animal power" was available. As for the lack of "simple machines," most simple machines in Europe and Asia before the eighteenth century depended on power from horses, oxen, water buffalo, mules, or cattle. All of these were unknown in the Americas. The authors didn't look for real explanations because white supremacy had convinced them ahead of time that these early nonwhites were probably dullards.

Beringia, Boats, or Both?

Many scholars still think that people reached the Americas by walking across the Beringia "land bridge." However, there is little archaeological evidence for this. And there is another possibility. More and more archaeologists think they came by boat.

Humans reached the island continent of Australia at least 40,000 years ago. They must have come by boat or raft. No matter how much ice piled up on land during the Ice Age, people could never have walked to Australia. It is separated from Asia by a deep ocean divide. Archaeologists have found no traces of boats older than 10,000 years—only stone tools have survived from that long ago. The lack of evidence of early boats doesn't mean that boats didn't exist. After all, nobody ever made stone boats!

Did humans reach the Americas by Beringia, by boat, or both? And did they come all at once or over a long period of time? Some scientists think that prehistoric people came to the Americas in waves, over thousands of years. Others think that modern Native Americans are descended from a single small band, based on their genetic similarities.

Textbooks could present these questions and invite kids to research them in the library and online. They could give students and teachers ideas about what to look for and how to weigh the evidence they find. If a yearlong American history class started this way, young people would realize right from the start that history still remains to be done. It is not just a mass of dead facts to be memorized.

"What Is Civilization?"

When textbooks talk about early societies in the Americas, they usually focus on whether people were "primitive" or "civilized."

These words have specific meanings in anthropology. To anthropologists, a primitive society has only a few different roles for people, such as mother, father, child, gatherer, and hunter. Even a religious leader may not have that as a full-time role. In a civilized society, on the other hand, some people are full-time healers, ministers, firefighters, even poodle clippers. The more roles, the more civilized! This scientific definition clashes with the way many people use "civilized"—to mean "polite," "refined," or "nice." To an anthropologist, Nazi Germany was highly civilized, but most nonscientists would not describe it that way.

Textbook authors confuse these two definitions of "civilization." One book said, "Those who planted seeds and cultivated the land instead of merely hunting and gathering food were more serene and comfortable." Another said, "These agricultural people were mostly peaceful, though they could fight fiercely to protect their fields. The hunters and gatherers, on the other hand, were quite warlike because their need to move about brought them frequently into contact with other groups."

Anthropologists, however, have found that most hunting and gathering societies were more peaceful than farming societies. Modern industrial societies have been still more warlike. The twentieth century, with its two world wars and countless other conflicts, proves that violence can increase along with civilization.

Most textbooks do point out that some Native American societies were civilized. The Aztecs and Mayans of Mexico and

Central America, and the Incas of South America, built cities and possessed wealth. In the eyes of the Spanish and other Europeans, this made them superior to other Native peoples. *The American Adventure* said, "Unlike the noncivilized peoples of the Caribbean, the Aztec were rich and prosperous."

Yet another textbook found plenty to criticize even in the rich and "advanced" Aztec and Inca civilizations. They hadn't "built ships to cross the oceans" or "reached out to the world. . . . [T]hey had ceased to progress. They were ripe for conquest." This is more bad history. The Aztec and Inca empires had grown swiftly in the century before the Spanish arrived. Here we see a form of blaming the victim. The thinking goes like this: Some peoples were conquered, so there must be reasons why the conquest was right, maybe even necessary. Let us come up with those reasons.

Unfortunately, even the best textbooks contrasted "primitive" Americans with "modern" Europeans. The books were really comparing rural America to urban Europe. This is like comparing the farming villages of the Massachusetts Indians to London, England's capital city. What if the countryside of Scotland were compared to Tenochtitlán, the Aztec capital, in 1491? Tenochtitlán was a city of between 100,000 and 300,000 people, with huge temples and markets. Scotland was mostly pastureland.

For a long time, Native Americans have questioned the way textbook authors use the term *civilized*. In 1927 a group of Native leaders said it was "unfair to the life of our people" that Europeans were so often called civilized, but American Indians were called savage or primitive. They went on to ask, "What is civilization? Its marks are a noble religion and philosophy, original arts, stirring music, rich story and legend. We had those. Then we are not savages, but a civilized race."

Three of the new books I surveyed did better than the rest at recognizing the diversity of Native American cultures. Textbooks found it harder, though, to explain how and why American Indian societies changed so quickly after contact with Europeans and Americans.

Most texts focused on just one group, the Plains Indians. Their culture flowered and changed after they acquired horses, which the Spanish had brought to the American West. This was syncretism—blending elements of two different cultures to create something new. But it was only a small part of what changed. Bigger changes took place as Europeans linked Native Americans to the growing world economy. Understanding these changes helps explain how Europeans took over North America.

A Tragic Reversal of Fortune

All along the eastern coast of the Americas, Native people traded with the Europeans. At first, Native Americans gave the English, French, and Dutch food in return for axes, blankets, cloth, beads, and kettles. Soon, though, Europeans persuaded the Native Americans to enter the fur trade and the slave trade. Natives were already better hunters and trappers than the Europeans. With guns the Europeans sold them, they became better still.

The Natives' way of life changed. Why spend hours weaving a watertight basket when it was faster to trap beavers that could be traded for a kettle? Why plant and tend your fields when it was easier to trade for food than to grow it?

Some of the rapid changes in eastern Indian societies were examples of syncretism. The Iroquois, for example, combined

> ## Ran away from his Master Nathanael Holbrook
> of Sherburn, on Wednesday the 19th of Sept last, an Indian Lad of
> about 18 Years of Age, named John Pittarne; He is pretty well sett
> and of a guilty Countenance and has short Hair; He had on a grey
> Coat with Pewter Buttons, Leather Breeches, an old tow Shirt,
> grey Stockings, good Shoes, and a Felt Hat.
>
> Whoever shall take up the said Servant, and convey him to
> his Master in Sherburn, shall have Forty Shillings Reward and all
> necessary Charges paid. We hear the said Servant intended to
> change his Name and his Clothes.

Like enslaved Africans, American Indians escaped when they could. This notice comes from the weekly Boston News-Letter *for October 4, 1739.*

their own fighting methods with European guns to smash their rivals, the Hurons. The Iroquois chose which parts of European culture to adopt, change, or ignore.

Not all changes were happy or voluntary. The Native Americans were under a military and cultural threat. Both sides knew that European guns were more efficient than American bows and arrows. The Europeans also realized that they could use trade goods to make alliances with the Native American nations they chose.

Tribes closest to the Europeans got guns first. Suddenly they had a great advantage over groups that did not have them. Native groups had fought among themselves before the Europeans came, but when guns were introduced, warfare increased. The European powers deliberately stepped up the conflict by playing Native nations against each other.

Natives in the North became deeply involved in the European fur trade. In the South, it was the slave trade. Many tribes were drawn into increased combat in order to enslave other Natives they could sell to the Europeans for more guns and kettles. Enslavement, like war, had existed among Native Americans long before the Europeans came. But like war, Indian slavery greatly increased once Europeans were involved.

European enslavement of Native Americans has a long history. Ponce de León didn't go to Florida to seek a mythical Fountain of Youth. His main business was looking for gold and slaves. In New England, Indian slavery led directly to African slavery. The first Africans were brought to New England in 1638 in exchange for Native Americans from Connecticut. When enslaved Native Americans and Africans in New York City united in a rebellion in 1712, one-fourth of the city's population was enslaved, and one-fourth of those enslaved were American Indians.

Among the colonies, South Carolina was the center of Native American slavery as well as African American slavery. In one year the colony shipped more than 10,000 Natives in chains to the West Indies. Whites in the Southwest enslaved Navajo and Apache people right up to the middle of the Civil War in the 1860s.

The increase in warfare and the slave trade made many established Native American settlements unsafe. To avoid being captured, people abandoned their cornfields and villages to live in smaller villages from which they could more easily escape to the woods. This meant that before long, they could not produce enough food and had to trade with the Europeans for it.

A tragic reversal of fortune took place. As Europeans learned from Natives what to grow and how to grow it, they needed

The textbook Life and Liberty *used images well to illustrate change in Native American societies. It showed students this pair of pictures and asked, "Which shows Indian life before Europeans arrived and which shows Indian life after? What evidence tells you the date?" In this way the textbook helped students understand that Europeans did not "civilize" or "settle" the "roaming" Natives. Instead, European horses allowed a less settled way of life for some Natives.*

less help from the Natives. At the same time, Natives came to depend more on Europeans for food and other goods. In the long run, it was the Natives who were enslaved, who died, and whose cultures fell apart.

Whites Who Chose Native Life

Our textbooks show a frontier line dividing whites and American Indians. As the white frontier moved forward, Indians moved back. This picture is incomplete. It fails to show how often, and how much, the two groups mingled and changed each other's societies. Instead of a moving line, the "frontier" was really a band or zone where whites, American Indians, and also blacks met and interacted.

The band of interaction was amazingly multicultural. In 1635, in the Dutch colony of New Amsterdam (later New York), sixteen different Native American, European, and African languages could be heard. In 1794, when the zone of contact had reached the eastern Midwest, a single town in northern Ohio had hundreds of Shawnee, Delaware, and Miami Indians; British and French traders and craftspeople; a few members of other Native groups; a few African and white captives; and whites who had married into or been adopted by Native families.

From the start, some whites and blacks had chosen to live with Native Americans, and many whites who were taken captive later stayed with them by choice. Benjamin Franklin said, "No European who has tasted Savage Life can afterwards bear to live in our societies."

Europeans were always trying to stop the flow of whites to Native societies. The Spanish explorer Hernando de Soto posted

Olive Oatman (1837–1903) was taken prisoner at the age of fourteen by Native Americans who had killed most other members of her family in Arizona. She soon passed into the hands of a Mojave group, who gave her the same tattoos they gave their daughters. After five years, during which she ignored several chances to return to white society, Olive agreed to be returned to a U.S. Army fort. There are conflicting accounts of her time with the Native Americans, and the full story will never be known, but Oatman, like many white "captives," felt affection and respect for the Natives with whom she had lived.

guards to keep his followers from running away. The Pilgrims were so worried about white people becoming Indianized that they made it a crime for men to wear long hair. Historian Karen Kupperman writes, "People who did run away to the Indians might expect very extreme punishments, even up to the death penalty," if they were caught by whites. Still, right up to the end of independent Native nations in 1890, white people continued to join them.

African Americans frequently fled to American Indian societies to escape enslavement. What was the attraction for whites? The main thing was probably the way Native societies were organized. As Franklin reported, "All their government is by the Counsel of Sages. There is no Force; there are no Prisons." Frontiersmen admired the freedom that Native Americans enjoyed as individuals. Women also had more status and power in most Native societies than in white societies of the time. In the seventeenth and eighteenth centuries, most of the American Indian groups in what is now the United States were much more democratic than Spain, France, or even England. Some historians think that Native ideas helped shape American democracy.

Learning Democracy from Native Americans

For 150 years, the Iroquois League was an example to the American colonies of how to govern a large territory in a democratic way. The League—also known as the Iroquois Confederacy or the Five Nations—formed when the Mohawk, Oneida, Onondaga, Cayuga, and Seneca tribes came together under a shared government in what is now New York State. When the Tuscarora joined, the League became known to Europeans as the Six Nations.

The League was governed by a council of representatives from each group. They spoke for the entire population and kept relations among the tribes peaceful. Throughout the colonial period, various European powers and settlements dealt with the Iroquois as a trading partner, ally, or enemy.

As a symbol of the new United States, Americans chose the eagle clutching a bundle of arrows. They knew that both the eagle and the arrows were symbols of the Iroquois League. Although one arrow is easily broken, no one can break six (or thirteen) at once.

In the 1740s the Iroquois got tired of dealing with several English colonies that often bickered among themselves. They suggested that the whites form a union similar to the Iroquois League. Benjamin Franklin, who had spent much time among the Iroquois and had seen their government in action, was enthusiastic. He drew up a plan for the colonies that he called the Albany Plan of Union, and he pleaded with colonial leaders to consider it, saying that if "six nations of ignorant savages" could make a long-lasting and effective union, surely "ten or a dozen English colonies" could do the same.

The colonies rejected the plan. Still, the Continental Congress, made up of representatives from the thirteen colonies who met in Philadelphia starting in 1774 to discuss self-government, openly mentioned Iroquois ideas. So did the

In the nineteenth century, Americans knew of Native contributions to medicine. 60% of all medicines patented in the century were marketed with American Indian images, including *Kickapoo Indian Cough Cure* and *Kickapoo Indian Oil.* In the twentieth century, Americans forgot or brushed aside the idea of Natives as healers.

Constitutional Convention of 1787, which created the U.S. Constitution. For a hundred years after the American Revolution, Native Americans were recognized as one source of our democratic institutions.

English and Dutch traditions also influenced the colonies, of course. American democracy seems to be another example of syncretism, combining ideas from Europe and Native America. The Native influence may not be proven by the strongest evidence, but textbooks should not leave it out.

But then, textbooks leave out most contributions of Native Americans to American culture. Many of the regional dishes Americans love combine Native, European, and African elements. Among these are New England pork and beans, New Orleans gumbo, and Texas chili. Dishes such as corn bread and grits, or greens and hush puppies, are part of African American soul food, but they also draw on American Indian traditions, because Indians and Africans were thrown together in bondage and also when blacks escaped to Native communities.

Some of what makes America different from Europe comes from Native American cultures. Yet to show Native American influence—especially in ideas—would require textbooks to be rewritten.

In 1970 the Indian Historical Press examined how textbooks treated Native Americans. One of the press's questions was, "Does the textbook describe the religions, philosophies, and contributions to thought of the American Indian?" Based on the textbooks I surveyed decades later, the answer was still no.

Native religions offer an example. Here is what one textbook in my survey said: "These Native Americans [in the Southeast] believed that nature was filled with spirits. Each form of life, such as plants and animals, had a spirit. Earth and air held spirits too. People were never alone. They shared their lives with the spirits of nature." This textbook was *trying* to show respect for Native religion, but it didn't work. Its flat statements made the beliefs seem like make-believe, not the sophisticated religious ideas of a higher civilization.

Suppose a textbook used the same simple tone and limited understanding to describe the beliefs of many Christians today. It might say, "These Americans believed that one great male god ruled the world. Sometimes they divided him into three parts, which they called father, son, and holy ghost. They ate crackers and wine or grape juice, believing that they were eating the son's body and drinking his blood. If they believed strongly enough, they would live on forever after they died."

No textbook would describe Christianity that way. It's offensive. Textbooks should present American Indian religions in a way that takes them seriously as complex, persuasive belief systems.

History Upside Down

What was the zone of contact like from the Native American side? Textbooks don't say much on the subject. They tend to focus on Indians such as Pocahontas and Squanto, who joined the invaders. They picture the white newcomers as "settlers," and they often present Natives as attackers or aggressors.

The American Way had this to say about the U.S. policy of forcing tribes to give up most of their land and retreat to reservations: "The United States Department of the Interior had tried to give each tribe both land and money." The textbook goes on to say that whites could not understand why the American Indians were not grateful: "To them, owning land was a dream come true." The truth is that whites of the time understood exactly why Indians were ungrateful. Said General Philip Sheridan, "We took away their country and their means of support, and it was for this and against this they made war. Could anyone expect less?"

The history books have turned history upside down. Let's try a right-side-up view: "After King Philip's War in the 1670s, there was continuous conflict at the edge of New England. In Vermont the settlers worried about savages scalping them." This is accurate—but only if the reader understands that the settlers were Native Americans and the scalpers were white.

Our textbooks do not challenge a long-standing archetype of our history: the picture of peaceful white settlers suffering occasional brutal attacks by American Indians. If they abandoned that archetype and gave a fuller, more balanced picture, it would become possible to understand why so many tribes turned to war, even when they knew they could not win.

War Stories

Our history is full of wars with Native American nations, but most of the original twelve textbooks I reviewed for *Lies* barely mentioned the topic. One of them listed the costs and battle deaths of "Major U.S. Wars." The list included no Indian wars. It had the Spanish-American War, with 385 dead, but not the Ohio War of 1790–95, which left 630 U.S. troops dead or missing after a single battle.

At least today's textbooks no longer blame Native Americans for the violence. The authors of the newer books are careful to admit that both sides acted with brutality. Some tell of the massacres of defenseless Native Americans by whites at Sand Creek, Colorado, and Wounded Knee, South Dakota.

For decades, movies and television showed wagon trains of white settlers attacked by savage American Indian hordes. In the real West, among 250,000 whites and blacks who traveled across the Plains between 1840 and 1860, only 362 pioneers died in all the recorded battles with American Indians. Those same encounters killed 426 Natives. It was much more common for Indians to help pioneers and new settlers. Indians gave the whites directions, showed them where to find water, sold them food or horses, and served as their guides and interpreters. But owing to our popular culture, young people have no idea that Natives considered European warfare far more savage than their own.

Indian Massacre at Wilkes-Barre *shows a common subject in nineteenth-century popular art: Natives invading the homes of white settlers. In reality, whites were invading Native lands and often Native homes, but pictures such as this one, not the reality, are the social archetype of Indian-settler relations.*

Most of the newer textbooks did cover New England's first Indian War, the Pequot War of 1636–37. The English colonists allied themselves with the Narragansetts. Together they attacked the Pequots, traditional enemies of the Narragansetts. Surrounding a Pequot village that held mostly women, children, and old men, the English set it on fire and shot those who tried to escape the flames. Pilgrim William Bradford described the scene:

> *It was a fearful sight to see them thus frying in the fire and the streams of blood quenching the same, and horrible was the stink and scent thereof; but the victory seemed a sweet sacrifice, and they gave praise thereof to God, who had wrought so wonderfully for them.*

The massacre shocked the Narragansetts. They had wanted to overpower the Pequots, not wipe them out. A captain of the English mocked their alarm. (Through the centuries, whites frequently complained that their Native allies did not fight hard enough.) The English colonists then tried to erase the memory of their victims. They even made it a crime to say the word *Pequot*.

At least our history books now tell how the English destroyed the Pequots. They also give space to King Philip's War, perhaps the most violent of the Indian wars, which erupted in 1675 when the English executed three Wampanoags and the Wampanoags responded by attacking. At the time, the fur trade that had linked the Europeans and Natives in Massachusetts was winding down. The Natives had already lost the land that had once supported them, and now they were losing the trade that had replaced it. By the end of the war, they had attacked 52 English villages. Twelve were destroyed. Relative to the population of the area, King Philip's War cost more lives—English and Native—than any other American war.

Our histories can hardly describe all of the Indian wars, because there were so many. But we must admit the Indian-ness of some of our *other* wars. From 1600 to 1754, Europe was often at war. These conflicts spread to the North American territories of the major European powers—England, France, and Spain. These powers fought mainly through their Native allies, who absorbed much of the conflict.

In North America the Seven Years War (1754–63), known in U.S. history as the French and Indian War, was fought mainly between Native Americans on the English and French sides. American Indians also fought in the American Revolution, the War of 1812, the Mexican War, and the Civil War. In each war, they fought mostly against other Natives. And in each war, the

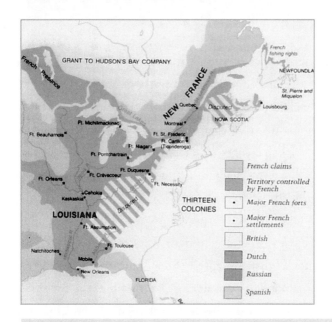

Most textbook maps, like the one above, show "French Territory," "British Territory," and so on, with no mention at all of American Indian territory. Maps that do show Native territory, such as the one below, highlight "conquest" of the Natives and show how they served as buffers between the European powers.

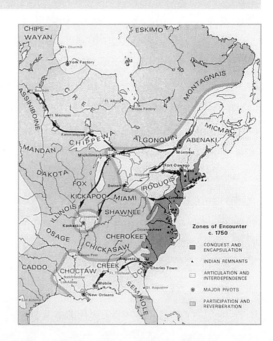

majority of Natives sided against the English, the colonies, and later the United States. They thought the other side would give them a better chance at keeping their land.

Land Changes Hands

The never-ending source of conflict between whites and Native Americans was land. Most textbooks I reviewed did state this, but they got other things wrong. Half of the textbooks, including some newer ones, repeated the old myth that American Indians had a childlike, primitive idea of land ownership that left them easily confused.

American Journey said that the Dutch "bought Manhattan from the Manhates people for a small amount of beads and other goods." What foolish Indians, not to recognize the potential of the island! Not one book pointed out that the Dutch paid the *wrong tribe* for Manhattan—or that what they paid was probably not beads at all, but more than $2,400 worth of metal kettles, blankets, guns, and steel knives and axes.

Europeans were forever paying the wrong tribe, or paying just a small group within a much larger nation. Often they didn't care—they simply wanted an excuse to take the land. The Europeans' fraudulent deals worked in their favor, because they frequently set one group of Natives against another.

The single biggest purchase from the wrong tribe took place in 1803, when President Thomas Jefferson made the Louisiana Purchase. All the textbooks in my survey told how Jefferson "doubled the size of the United States by buying Louisiana from France." Not one pointed out that it was not France's land to sell. The French did not consult with the Native owners of the land. Most Native Americans never even knew about the sale. France did not really sell the Louisiana Purchase territory to the United States. It merely sold its *claim* to the territory. The United States was still paying American Indian tribes for the purchase through most of the nineteenth century—and fighting them for it, as well.

Even some recent textbooks made the Natives appear stupid for not understanding that when they sold their land, they transferred not just the right to farm it but other rights as well. In the words of one text, "To Native Americans, no one owned the land—it was there for everyone to use." Nonsense! American Indians and Europeans had about the same views of land ownership, except that most Indians did not think that individuals could buy or sell land. Only whole villages could do that. And most Natives who made treaties to sell their land kept the rights to hunt, fish, or travel on it.

Better Histories

Could the history of whites and Native Americans have taken a different path? Of course. But the alternatives to war are like roads that were not taken. The past was full of possibilities that historians can point out. When it came to dealing with American Indians, white Americans had choices. They were often divided among themselves. What are some roads that might have been taken but weren't?

Whites and Native Americans might have existed together peacefully. From the start, whites made this impossible. For example, around Plymouth the American Indians leased their grazing land to the whites but kept their planting land. Colonists

Who Lost the War of 1812?

Textbooks used to say that the War of 1812, between Great Britain and the United States, came about because Britain refused to show respect to U.S. ships and seamen. This was the excuse that President James Madison's administration gave for the war. Newer textbooks tell the truth: that the war mostly grew out of conflict with Indians over land.

All along the boundary between white settlement and Native territory, whites wanted to push farther into Indian country. States along the frontier elected representatives who went to Washington to urge a war that frontier whites wanted. Because the British were seen as supporting the American Indians, the war was with Britain—but most of it was fought along the frontier. The United States fought seven major land battles in the War of 1812. Five were fought mainly against Native Americans.

Most textbooks I examined entirely missed the most significant result of the war. One of them, *The American Adventure*, stated it correctly and directly: "The American Indians were the only real losers of the war." In return for the United States leaving Canada alone, Great Britain gave up its alliances with Native Americans throughout the territories that were later made part of the United States. This changed U.S.-Indian relations forever. The Indian wars that came afterward cost thousands of lives on both sides, but they never again amounted to a serious threat to the United States.

Another result of the War of 1812 was the loss of part of our history. As historian Bruce Johansen put it, "A century of learning [from Native Americans] was coming to a close. A century and more of forgetting—of calling history into service to rationalize conquest—was beginning." Even the meaning of *American* changed. Before 1815, it was generally used to refer to Native Americans. After 1815, it meant European Americans.

"Come over and help us," a Native pleads (to white Europeans) on the official seal of the Massachusetts Bay Colony. This white settler propaganda became an archetype: well-meaning Europeans and tragically different Natives. Textbooks that say that Natives were unwilling or unable to become part of American culture keep that false archetype alive.

let their livestock run free and destroy Indian crops. When trouble broke out over this, the colonial courts sided with the whites. They held that Natives were not citizens and therefore lacked legal rights. This pattern prevented whites and Indians from living in peaceful equality. Harmonious communities made up of white, black, and Indian people did form, but they were small and usually isolated from the larger society.

Another road not taken was the creation of an American Indian state within the United States. The Delaware Indians suggested this in 1778. They were turned down. In the 1840s, Indian Territory wanted to send representatives to Congress, as white territories did. White Southerners blocked this idea. There was never a sincere plan to give Native Americans statehood.

Textbooks tend to dwell on another road—one that was doomed to fail. That road was total acculturation, which means that Native Americans were supposed to completely blend into white society. The view usually given in textbooks is that acculturation failed because American Indians were tragically unable or unwilling to adopt white ways.

The truth is that white Americans did not really want Indians to acculturate. Sometimes they made this clear. In 1789, for example, Massachusetts made it illegal to teach Natives to read and write "under penalty of death." At other times, whites met Indians' concerns with meaningless words. President Thomas Jefferson did this in 1808, advising a group of Cherokees to

In the early nineteenth century, the Cherokee in Georgia owned mills, livestock, and blacksmith shops. Some were wealthy planters. One of them, Joseph Vann, owned 300 acres of land, several businesses—and this mansion. It aroused the envy of the sheriff and other whites, who kicked Vann out in 1834 and took the house for themselves.

settle down on the land they had been given and become farmers. In reality, the Cherokees *were* farmers. They had visited Jefferson to ask him to assign the land to them as individuals and to make them citizens.

No matter how well Native Americans acculturated, they could not succeed in white society. Whites would not let them. Indians who gained property or wealth, built European-style houses, or ran businesses became targets of white thugs who wanted to take over their property. Most courts simply refused to hear testimony from Native Americans against whites. Acculturation could not work because American Indians were not given equal legal rights.

Presenting Indian history as a tragedy because Native Americans could not or would not acculturate is feel-good history for whites. So is downplaying the Indian wars, which helps us forget that we took the continent from its inhabitants. Wars between whites and Natives dominated our history from 1622 to 1815. They remained significant until 1890. But they have mostly disappeared from our national memory.

The answer is not to tell Indian history as a parade of white villains. History is more complex than that. Textbooks are beginning to reveal some of the divisions among whites that could have changed the direction of Native-white relations. Most textbooks now mention the titanic struggle between John Marshall, chief justice of the Supreme Court, and President Andrew Jackson over Jackson's wish to drive the Cherokees out of Georgia. The court's decision supported the Cherokees, but Jackson ignored it. He used military force to drive them out of their homeland, a journey they call the Trail of Tears. Textbooks could go further, however. They could point out that some political and religious groups urged the public to support fair play for the Cherokees.

Native American artists have found ways to become both modern and Native. In the 1930s, Inuit artists in Canada began carving soapstone, a material that their ancestors had used for making pots. Nalenik Temela's sculpture Dancing to My Spirit *is a beautiful example of syncretism—the blending of cultures to form something new.*

Most new textbooks do a good job of explaining the American Indian Movement (AIM), which in the early 1970s briefly took over Alcatraz Island in San Francisco, the Bureau of Indian Affairs in the nation's capital, and Wounded Knee in South Dakota. Native Americans want textbooks to recognize that after all the wars, plagues, and pressures against their cultures, American Indians still survive. They still engage in government-to-government relations with the United States.

More than that, Native Americans want to be seen as more than stereotypes. They are not frozen in a traditional "way of life" as whites imagine they existed at the time of first contact with whites. Native peoples of that time did not have a "way of life." They had many. Their cultures have changed since then, as all cultures do.

Like other populations, American Indians are syncretic, adopting elements from other cultures. If our histories were better at showing syncretism in both directions, if we were more aware of the effect of American Indian ideas on our overall culture, the United States might see the value in continuing to learn from Native American societies.

Chapter 5

INVISIBLE RACISM

The black-white rift stands at the very center of American history. . . . If we forget that—if we forget the great stain of slavery that stands at the heart of our country, our history, our experiment—we forget who we are, and we make the great rift deeper and wider.

—Ken Burns

RACE IS THE SHARPEST AND DEEPEST DIVISION IN American life. The domination of black America by white America, and the conflict over racial slavery, may be the most important theme in American history.

Writer and historian Studs Terkel called race our "American obsession." He was right. Our society has repeatedly been torn apart, and sometimes bound together, by the issue of race relations. Among other things, race has shaped and reshaped our political parties.

Before the 1850s, the United States had two political parties, the Democrats and the Whigs. The Whig Party fell apart over the question of whether or not to support slavery. A new party, the Republicans, took the antislavery position. Abraham Lincoln was its first president. A year after he was assassinated, the Republicans passed a Civil Rights Act in 1866 over the wishes of President Andrew Johnson, a Democrat. They promoted the rights of African Americans after the Civil War.

In contrast, many Democrats were antiblack. The Democratic Party labeled itself the "white man's party" for almost a century. Beginning in 1964, sweeping changes in the parties led the American people to shift their loyalties. People of color turned increasingly toward the Democratic Party. The white South, once largely Democratic, became a Republican stronghold.

Even when our textbooks cover race-related subjects, they generally ignore the underlying *reason* for racial struggle. That reason is white supremacy—the belief that whites are better or smarter than others. It has given rise to prejudice, unequal treatment, and violence. Yet the struggle has also inspired resistance and change.

Stories White America Has Told

Over the years white America has told itself stories about the enslavement of blacks. For two centuries, the most popular novel in the United States was set in slavery. In the nineteenth century, that novel was *Uncle Tom's Cabin*, by Harriet Beecher Stowe. In the twentieth, it was *Gone with the Wind*, by Margaret Mitchell.

The two books tell very different stories. In *Uncle Tom's Cabin*, slavery is an evil to be fought against. *Gone with the Wind* suggests that slavery was a gracious social structure, something to be mourned when it passed. Until the civil rights movement, twentieth-century textbooks in American history pretty much agreed with Margaret Mitchell. My own high-school textbook presented enslavement as not such a bad thing. If bondage was

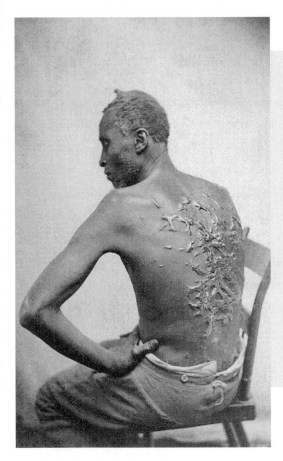

An enslaved African American known as Gordon escaped in 1863 from a Louisiana plantation. He reached U.S. lines and in April stripped to the waist for a physical examination so he could join the army. He had been whipped the previous October. This photo of his scarred back became internationally known as a symbol of the cruelties of slavery.

a burden for African Americans, well, at least they were happy and well fed.

This is a myth. It says that slavery did no real harm to anyone, white or black. Fortunately, it is not what textbooks say today. Since the civil rights movement of 1955–70, they have turned back toward Harriet Beecher Stowe's picture of slavery as inhumane, unjust, and cruel.

Today's textbooks also show how slavery dominated more and more of the nation's political life in the first half of the nineteenth century. They tell how slavery expanded into new territories and states as the government pushed Native Americans out of their lands. They tell how slave owners, who once apologized for slavery as an economically necessary evil, put in place harsh new laws and customs. One textbook reports, "Talk of freeing the slaves became more and more dangerous in the South."

Even to receive abolitionist literature in the mail became a crime in some slaveholding states. Legal protection for African Americans who were already free became shaky, even in the North. Meanwhile, the antislavery activists—called abolitionists because they wanted to abolish, or do away with, slavery— grew more and more unhappy. They were disgusted that their nation had lost its idealism. The debate over slavery grew larger. And then came secession, in which a string of Southern states left the Union.

States Chose Slavery

The first state to secede from the Union was South Carolina. Its leaders were perfectly clear about why they were seceding. On Christmas Eve they signed a "Declaration" of their reasons. The biggest reason was that some Northern states had found loopholes and ways around a federal law called the Fugitive Slave Act of 1850.

The Fugitive Slave Act said that people enslaved in Southern slave states did not become free when they entered Northern free states. Special courts set up by the national government enforced the return of the fugitives to slavery, sometimes against the wishes of local communities. Northern states, however, had found ways to interfere with the Fugitive Slave Act. This angered the leaders of South Carolina, who were also upset that some Northerners had called slavery "sinful" and openly allowed abolitionist groups to form.

In addition, South Carolina was upset because some Northern states let African Americans vote and become citizens. This was none of South Carolina's business. At the time, states decided who could vote. The Fifteenth Amendment to the Constitution, which says that the federal and state governments cannot prevent a person from voting based on "race, color, or previous condition of servitude," did not become law until 1870, well after the Civil War. Another grievance for South Carolina was that the new Republican Party, formed in opposition to slavery, had just won the presidency.

So South Carolinians were angry because free states had chosen not to return people who had escaped from enslavement, had allowed criticism of slavery, and had let blacks have some rights. In short, South Carolina was against the rights of states to make their own laws—when those laws threatened slavery or white supremacy. Keep that in mind when you see the phrase "states' rights" later in this section. Other states that seceded echoed South Carolina. Mississippi, for example, said, "Our position is thoroughly identified with the institution of slavery."

The states that had seceded formed their own government, called the Confederacy. Its leaders wrote a new constitution that protected enslavement at the federal level. It did not allow states to be antislavery or to secede from the Confederacy. Slavery was clearly more important to the Confederates than states' rights.

Secession had a deeper cause as well: white supremacy. Many white Southerners feared disaster, even race war, if the 4,000,000 African Americans in their midst were freed. For this reason, even some Southerners who did not own human property rallied to protect the institution of slavery.

In spite of clear evidence about why the states seceded, many textbooks before 1970 gave any cause *but* slavery for secession.

They pointed to disagreements over taxes and tariffs, conflict between the farming South and the industrial North, and especially states' rights. They claimed the South supported states' rights and felt the Union had trampled on them. These new versions of secession made the South look better than the truth would have done, but they were bad history.

After the civil rights movement, most textbook authors changed their positions on why the South seceded. They came to agree with Abraham Lincoln, who said in his second inaugural speech, "All knew that [slavery] was somehow the cause of the war." As one 1981 textbook put it, "At the center of the conflict was slavery, the issue that would not go away."

Most textbooks now handle the topic of slavery with depth and understanding—with one important exception. To my surprise, the newest textbooks in my survey backtracked on the question of what caused secession. Some returned to the old explanation of states' rights. One of these said, "Southerners justified secession with the theory of states' rights." Another explained the South's position with a quote from Jefferson Davis, president of the Confederacy, who said that the South fought to "obtain respect for the rights [to] which we were entitled." The authors did not say *what* rights Davis meant, leaving everything vague.

Surprised by Slavery

Americans seem to be continually startled by slavery. Very few people today realize that our society has known legal enslavement far longer than it has been free. Even fewer know that slavery was not limited to the South. It was important in the North until after the Revolutionary War.

Massachusetts was the first colony to make slavery legal. In New York, Wall Street was the marketplace where owners could hire out their enslaved workers by the day or week. The city had a population of 7,000 people in 1720. Sixteen hundred of them were African Americans, and most of those were enslaved. But

Most Founding Fathers Owned People

Children are shocked to learn that George Washington and Thomas Jefferson kept slaves. In 2003 an Illinois teacher told her students that most presidents before Lincoln were slaveholders. Her students were outraged—not with the presidents, but with her, for lying to them.

"That's not true," they said, "or it would be in the book!" They meant their textbook, which had many pages about Washington, Jefferson, Madison, Jackson, and other early presidents but said not one word about their owning enslaved men, women, and children. Textbooks cannot bear to reveal anything bad about their heroes.

After the students did some research and convinced themselves that their teacher was right, they wrote letters to the author and publisher of that textbook. The author never replied. Someone at the publisher sent a letter thanking the students for "useful feedback on our product." By failing to take their point seriously, the publisher let these young people know that no one was paying attention.

Our Founding Fathers and their families wrestled with slavery. Patrick Henry, for example, is remembered for his passionate "Give me liberty or give me death" speech. He owned people, even adding to them throughout the Revolutionary period. Unlike some other Virginia planters, he set none of them free. Henry himself saw that his actions did not match his words. He exclaimed, "Would anyone believe I am the master of slaves of my own purchase?" Of all the textbooks I examined, only two mention this about Henry.

most textbooks downplay slavery in the North. Slavery then comes to look like a regional problem, not a national one.

Textbooks do now show the horror of slavery and its effect on black America. But they don't say much about how slavery affected *white* America, North or South. In fact, textbooks have trouble admitting that anything might be wrong with white Americans or with the United States as a whole.

Perhaps being more honest about what slavery was like for enslaved individuals was the easy part. After all, slavery is dead. We have moved beyond it, so we can talk about its evils. But that is hollow and meaningless unless we can also talk about what enslavement means to us in the present moment.

Slavery left two legacies for the present. One is that it placed African Americans in a position of inferiority, both socially and economically. The other is that it bred racism in whites. Both of these legacies still haunt our society. Treating the legacies of slavery is controversial because, unlike slavery, racism is not over yet.

Roots of Racism

Racism in the Western world stems mainly from two activities that unfolded through history and were related to each other. One is the taking of land by Europeans from the peoples who lived on it, and the destruction of those peoples. The other is enslaving Africans to work that land. Slavery and racism reinforced each other.

Slavery was a social and economic system that existed in many places and times. The slavery started by Europeans in the fifteenth century was different, because it was the enslavement of one *race* by another. As time went on, Europeans came to see the enslavement of white people as wrong, while the enslavement of black people became acceptable, even "natural." Unlike earlier slaveries, children of enslaved African Americans would be enslaved forever. They could never gain freedom by marrying into the owning class.

Racism was the system of ideas that supported this different treatment. Whites molded their ideas about blacks—that they were unequal beings, subhuman, even animals—in order to justify the social and economic system that relied on the new form of racial slavery. The French philosopher Montesquieu understood this when in 1748 he said, ironically, "It is impossible for us to believe these creatures to be men, because, allowing them to be men, a suspicion would follow that we ourselves are not Christian."

Historians have tracked the rise of racism in the West. Before the 1450s, Europeans saw Africans as different but not necessarily inferior. As more nations joined the slave trade, Europeans began to think of Africans as stupid, backward, and uncivilized. Amnesia set in. Conveniently, Europeans forgot things they had long known, such as that Timbuktu, a city in what is now the African nation of Mali, was a center of learning with a famous university and library. Now Europeans—and European Americans—saw Africa as the "dark continent" and its people as savages.

By the 1850s, many white Americans, including Northerners, claimed that black people were so hopelessly inferior that slavery was a proper form of "education" for them. Enslavement also did Africans the favor of taking them away from the "dark continent."

The social and economic system of slavery died with the Civil War in the middle of the nineteenth century. The idea system of racism, however, has lived on. The essence of what we have inherited from slavery is the idea that it is right, even "natural," for whites to be on top, blacks on the bottom. Our culture tells all of us, including African Americans, that Europe's domination of the world came about because (white) Europeans were smarter. This message is white supremacy. It is driven home in so many ways that many whites and even some people of color believe it.

White supremacy is not just left over from slavery. Since slavery ended, other developments in American history have maintained it. Textbooks, however, do not explore this topic. Only one in my survey connected history and racism. It did so in just half a sentence, saying that slaveholders' fears of an uprising led to "an intoxicating theory of racial superiority." If students aren't asked to think about what causes racism, they may conclude that it's "natural." But it isn't. Racism is a result not of biology, but of history.

Slavery Undercut Democracy

The idealism in the American Revolution made the United States a symbol and supporter of democracy around the world—at first. Then slavery and racism weakened our Revolutionary idealism.

After the Revolution, many Americans expected our example to inspire other peoples. It did. In the 1790s, the black population of Haiti rose up in revolution against France, which controlled Haiti as a colony. Our young nation got its first chance to help an oppressed people in a struggle for freedom. Which side did we help: white French plantation owners, or rebellious Haitians trying to build a free black republic?

President George Washington owned people. His administration loaned hundreds of thousands of dollars to the planters. The next president, John Adams, did not own people. His administration supported the Haitians. Our third president, Thomas Jefferson, owned people. In 1801, he reversed U.S. policy toward Haiti and secretly gave France permission to retake the island.

Planters in the United States were scared by the Haitian Revolution. They thought it would inspire slave revolts here. (It did.) When the Haitians won anyway, the United States refused to send diplomats to the island. Not one of the eighteen textbooks in my survey told of our flip-flop on supporting the Haitians.

Racial slavery also shaped our policy when Spain's colonies in the Americas began to revolt. U.S. statesmen had mixed feelings. On one hand, they liked the idea of booting a European power out of the Americas. On the other hand, they were worried because the rebels who were doing the booting were racially mixed. Some American planters and diplomats wanted the United States to replace Spain as a colonial power in the Americas. Instead of visions of democratic liberty for the Americas, slavery led the United States to consider building its own empire.

Between 1787 and 1855 the United States grew by adding new territories on its western border. This was driven in large part by the influence of slaveholders. The largest pressure group behind the War of 1812 was made up of slaveholders who wanted land that was claimed by American Indians and by Spain. They also wanted to drive Native societies farther away from the slaveholding states so that black people would have nowhere to run.

Florida was a Spanish territory, but it changed hands because of slave owners' pressure. Spain played no real part in the War of 1812, but afterward the United States took Florida from Spain because slave owners demanded we do so.

The Longest Indian War

The longest Indian war in American history was fought over African Americans.

Before the Europeans and Africans arrived, the Seminoles did not exist as a tribe or a nation. Afterward, they came together in the Florida Everglades as a society made up of Creek Indians, survivors of smaller tribes, runaway slaves, and whites who chose to live among them.

The Seminoles refused to turn over the fugitive slaves who had joined them. Because of this, they were attacked twice. Whites did not make war on the Seminoles because they wanted their land. The Everglades had no economic value to the United States in the nineteenth century. Whites wanted to do away with a refuge for escaped slaves.

The First Seminole War lasted from 1816 to 1818. The Second Seminole War lasted from 1835 to 1842, making it our longest Indian war. Five of the six newer history textbooks I reviewed mentioned this war. Only one came close to telling that ex-slaves were the real reason for it.

Slavery was also behind the Texas War of 1835–36. Davy Crockett, Jim Bowie, and others who fought at the Alamo became heroes of American popular culture. They fought for freedom—but it was the freedom to own other people. Our next major war was the Mexican War of 1846–48. Again, it was driven by Southern planters who wanted to push the border of the nearest free land farther from the slave states.

Racism Remains Invisible

For our first 70 years as a nation, slavery tilted our foreign policy more toward empire building than toward self-determination for other peoples. Textbooks cannot show this unless they are willing to talk about ideas like racism, which might make whites look bad. So racism remains invisible in textbook treatments of our relations with other countries. What about domestic policy—our decisions and actions within our own borders?

Racism remains invisible there, too. One example is the series of seven debates between Stephen A. Douglas and Abraham Lincoln in 1858. Douglas was the most important leader of the Democratic Party at the time. He had been a U.S. senator from Illinois since 1847, and he had hopes of becoming president. Lincoln had represented Illinois in the U.S. House of Representatives from 1847 to 1849. In 1858 the Republican Party chose him to run for senator against Douglas.

Douglas claimed to be neither for nor against slavery, although most of his money came from a plantation in Mississippi. However, he had pushed through Congress a bill that opened new territories to slavery, north and west of Missouri. The result was war between proslavery and "free soil," or antislavery, groups in Kansas. When Lincoln faced Douglas in the debates, the contest was between rival ideas that would dominate the Republican and Democratic Parties for years to come.

The textbooks in my survey gave an average of seven paragraphs and two pictures to the Lincoln-Douglas debates, but all twelve older books included a total of just three sentence fragments of Douglas's actual words. As a result, readers couldn't tell where Douglas actually stood.

The newer textbooks did a little better, but not much. Four of them at least said that the debates had something to do with slavery. They should have gone further. The debates were largely about slavery and the position African Americans would eventually hold in our society. Douglas made his position clear:

"In my opinion this government of ours is founded on the white basis. It was made by the white man, for the benefit of the white man, to be administered by white men."

Even the newest textbooks I examined gave no hint of Douglas's racism. Why did textbooks censor his views? They gave all sorts of unimportant details, so they had plenty of room to quote his racism. The heroification process seems to be operating again. Douglas's words might make us think badly of him. So let's leave them out.

Most textbooks also protect us from a racist Lincoln. This complex subject is covered in chapter 6, but here is what Lincoln said in one of the debates: "I am not, nor ever have been in favor of bringing about the social and political equality of the white and black races [applause]—that I am not nor ever have been in favor of making voters or jurors of Negroes."

By shielding students from such truths, textbook authors make it harder for young people to see racism as a force in American life. For if Lincoln could be racist, then so might the rest of us be. And if he could rise above racism, as he did at times, then so might the rest of us.

Reconstruction Reality

When the Union won and the Civil War ended in 1865, Democrats were the minority party. Republicans controlled the Reconstruction period, from 1865 to 1877, when the federal government supervised Southern elections.

Right after the war, Southern states under their old Confederate leaders passed laws called "black codes" to limit the freedoms and rights of African Americans, including those newly

Reconstruction gave African Americans new political power—
for a while. Top: Black men, one of whom is a soldier, cast their
first votes. Bottom: Voters elected African Americans to positions in government.

freed from slavery. This brought a backlash in the North. The *Chicago Tribune*, the most important voice of the Republican Party in the Midwest, declared, "We tell the white men of Mississippi that the men of the North will convert the state of Mississippi into a frog pond before they will allow any such laws to disgrace one foot of soil in which the bones of our soldiers sleep and over which the flag of freedom waves."

The Republican Party took the lead in passing federal laws—and sending federal troops into the South—to guarantee blacks' rights and help them get started in their new lives. African Americans were elected to state legislatures across the South and also to the U.S. Congress.

Reconstruction's interracial democracy was a success, but it didn't last long. White racism and resentment still existed, and not just in the South. Support for Reconstruction weakened. Democrats fought to regain control. So did violent organizations such as the Ku Klux Klan and other white supremacist groups. By 1877, the Democrats had won back all the Southern state legislatures. Reconstruction was over. (Chapter 6 has more on the successes of early Reconstruction.)

History textbooks written after Reconstruction often reflected the views of those who had defeated it. Between about 1890 and 1960, they painted an unattractive—and inaccurate—picture of heavy-handed Republican rule during Reconstruction. We might call this the neo-Confederate myth of Reconstruction. For a while, African American families kept the truth of Reconstruction alive. Then, as people who had lived through the period died off, the textbook view took hold even in the black community.

My most memorable meeting with the Confederate myth of Reconstruction happened in 1969, at a mostly black school, Tou-

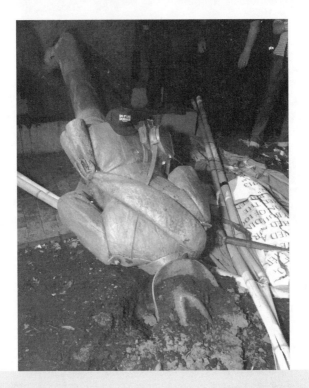

In August 2018, protestors toppled "Silent Sam," a Confederate statue. Despite protests against its glorification of the Confederacy and the slavery it represented, he had stood at the main entrance of the University of North Carolina for more than a century. After the statue's removal, university officials debated whether to restore it. A better solution might be to leave it lying, with a plaque explaining its history and why it was toppled.

galoo College in Mississippi. I was about to start teaching a unit on Reconstruction. On the first day of class, I asked my seventeen first-year students what they already knew. Sixteen of them said: Reconstruction was the time when African Americans took over the Southern states, including Mississippi. But slavery had just ended, and blacks didn't know how to govern. They messed up and reigned corruptly. Whites had to take back control.

I sat stunned. African Americans never took over the Southern states. All the governors were white. All but one of the state

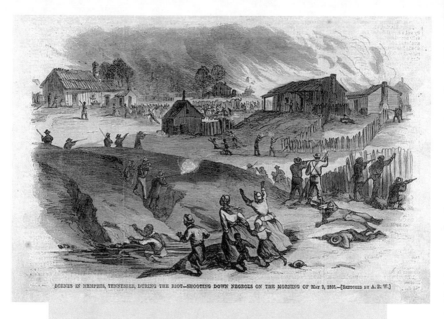

SCENES IN MEMPHIS, TENNESSEE, DURING THE RIOT—SHOOTING DOWN NEGROES ON THE MORNING OF May 2, 1866.—[SKETCHED BY A. R. W.]

In 1866, armed whites raided a black neighborhood in Memphis, Tennessee. In just this single case of racial violence during and after Reconstruction, 40 African Americans died, and whites burned down every black church and school in the city.

legislatures had white majorities throughout Reconstruction. Moreover, the Reconstruction governments did not "mess up." Mississippi, in particular, had better government during Reconstruction than in the decades that followed. And "whites" did not take back control of the state governments. *Some* white Democrats used force and fraud to seize control from Republican governments that included people of both races.

For young African Americans to believe such a harmful myth about their past was tragic. It invited them to believe that their race had "messed up" its primary appearance on the center stage of history, and so it was right for whites to be in control. Yet my students had only learned what their textbooks had taught them. History had been a weapon, used against them.

Today's textbooks have vastly improved their treatment of Reconstruction. They no longer claim that federal troops controlled Southern society for a decade or more. Now they point out that military rule ended in all but three states by 1868. They give a much more accurate picture of the successes of Reconstruction legislatures in the South.

Textbook accounts of Reconstruction have improved, but some of their pictures have not. Seven of the eighteen books I examined for this book used this cartoon, in which "The Solid South" is a delicate white woman carrying the heavy burden of President Ulysses S. Grant and his weapons stuffed into a carpetbag and held in place by blue-coated soldiers of occupation. Only two of the textbooks asked students to interpret the cartoon.

Textbooks now show African Americans striving to improve their lives after the Civil War. But the authors still miss the key point: the problem of Reconstruction was bringing Confederates, not African Americans, into the new order.

The 50-Year Low Point

To properly understand Reconstruction, we must look at white racism. And that becomes even more necessary to understanding the period from 1890 to 1940. African American historian Rayford Logan called this period "the nadir of American race relations." *Nadir* means "the lowest point," and it was. During the nadir, African Americans were put back into second-class citizenship. White Americans, North and South, joined hands to put them there.

Most of the textbooks in my survey provided some twigs about the nadir, without giving an overview of the forest. One of them summed it up in these lifeless words: "Reconstruction left many major problems unsolved and created new and equally urgent problems. This was true even though many forces in the North and the South continued working to reconcile the two sections."

These sentences are so vague that they are meaningless. Journalist and historian Frances FitzGerald used an earlier version of that same passage to attack what she called the "problems" approach to American history. "These 'problems' seem to crop up everywhere," FitzGerald wrote. "History in these texts is a mass of problems."

Five hundred pages later, the same textbook reached the civil rights movement of the mid-twentieth century. Race relations

FRANCHISE.
AND NOT THIS MAN?

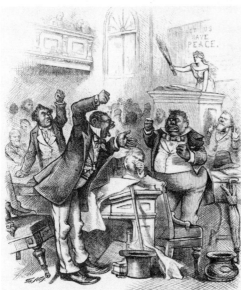

COLORED RULE IN A RECONSTRUCTED (?) STATE.—(See Page 244.)
(THE MEMBERS CALL EACH OTHER THIEVES, LIARS, RASCALS AND COWARDS.)
COLUMBIA. "You are Aping the lowest Whites. If you disgrace your Race in this way you had better take Back Seats."

Two cartoons by Thomas Nast mirror the revival of racism in the North after the Civil War. "And Not This Man?" (top) appeared in Harper's Weekly in 1865. It shows the artist's commitment to black voting soon after the war. Nine years later, as Reconstruction was winding down, Nast's images of African Americans show the rise of racism. "Colored Rule in a Reconstructed (?) State" was published in 1874, also in Harper's. It mocked the idea of African Americans as lawmakers at a time when whites in the North were thinking about giving up on black civil rights.

The Changing Face
of Uncle Tom

Popular culture is like a mirror held up to society. As white America chipped away at the civil and political rights of African Americans, our popular culture started treating them differently, too. The Bronx Zoo, for example, picked up on the old racist archetype that blacks were inferior humans, or even animals. It displayed an African behind bars, like a gorilla.

The change shows up clearly in theatrical productions based on the famous novel *Uncle Tom's Cabin*. The novel was a criticism of slavery. In it, the character Tom was an enslaved man who gave his life to protect his people. That wouldn't do for a society that was becoming increasingly racist. The story was rewritten for the stage to turn Tom into a sentimental dope who was loyal to his kind white masters. In the black community, *Uncle Tom* eventually came to mean an African American without integrity, someone who goes along with whites and sells out his own people's interests.

In the 1880s and 1890s, minstrel shows became wildly popular from New England to California. These featured white actors in blackface, made up to look like caricatures of African Americans who came across as bumbling fools. These shows presented images of African Americans who had been happy on the plantation. Once off it, they were lost, and bad at everything.

Minstrel songs also sold that misty vision of the happy plantation. "Carry Me Back to Old Virginny," "Old Black Joe," and "My Old Kentucky Home" told whites that Harriet Beecher Stowe, the author of *Uncle Tom's Cabin*, had gotten it all wrong. Blacks really *liked* slavery. Second-class citizenship was all they deserved.

again became a "problem." In this approach to history, nothing ever causes anything. Things just happen. The authors of that textbook never tried to connect the failure of the United States to guarantee black civil rights in 1877 with the need for a civil rights movement almost a century later.

Between 1890 and 1907 every Southern state passed laws that let them take voting rights away from most African American voters. Lynchings—public murders, with considerable support from the community—rose to an all-time high. Most of the victims were black. In 1896 the U.S. Supreme Court ruled that racial segregation was legal.

Unfortunately, the textbooks I researched mostly got segregation wrong. They pointed out that the "separate but equal" schools, buses, parks, hospitals, and other facilities provided for African Americans were rarely "equal." But segregation's essence was the separation of races itself. *Segregation* is a system of rules and customs that keeps races separate when they are doing equal tasks, such as learning the multiplication tables, but allows them to be close when the dominant race is giving orders to the other, such as a white employer and a black cook or maid. Requiring the separation in and of itself carries the meaning that the "lower" group is inferior and must be kept away from "normal" people.

During the nadir, segregation increased everywhere. We celebrate baseball player Jackie Robinson for breaking the color barrier in his sport, but Robinson was not the first black player in major-league baseball. African Americans had played in the major leagues in the nineteenth century, but by 1889 whites had driven them out.

In the North as well as the South, whites forced blacks from skilled jobs and even unskilled ones, such as delivering mail.

From the Civil War to the end of the nineteenth century, not a single Democrat, from North or South, voted in favor of any civil rights law. The new discrimination faced by African Americans was national, not just Southern. For example, Northern universities such as Harvard no longer let African Americans into their dormitories, although they could still attend classes.

Riots, Rules, and Reactions

Chapter 1 of this book tells how President Woodrow Wilson segregated the federal government. It also describes Wilson's admiration for the movie *Birth of a Nation*. That movie helped the Ku Klux Klan grow to more than 4,000,000 members. For a time the KKK openly dominated the state governments of Georgia, Indiana, Oklahoma, and Oregon. It is even likely that President Warren G. Harding became a KKK member in a ceremony at the White House.

Maybe as many as 100 race riots took place during Wilson's and Harding's presidencies. In these rampages, white mobs killed African Americans. One such riot took place in 1921 in Tulsa, Oklahoma. Whites dropped dynamite from planes onto the main black business and residential area, killing 75 people and destroying more than 1,100 homes.

It is almost unimaginable how racist the United States became during the nadir. From Florida to Oregon, whites attacked their black neighbors, driving them out and leaving entire towns all white. Most of these riots have vanished from our history. Communities with no black residents passed laws—or just made plans—to threaten African Americans with death if they stayed in town overnight. Thousands of communi-

ALL WHITE HELP!

BILL & REX
MOVING SERVICE
226-1999

CALL TODAY!

ties became "sundown towns," because black people had better leave before sundown if they knew what was good for them.

African Americans were kept off juries throughout the South and in some parts of the North. This meant they could forget about legal justice, even when they were the victims of crimes such as assault, theft, or arson by whites. Lynchings symbolized how defenseless blacks were in state courts. Yet for decades the United States could not pass a federal law against lynching. In December 2018 the U.S. Senate finally approved a bill that called lynching "the ultimate expression of racism in the United States following Reconstruction" and would make lynching a federal hate crime.

Unable to overcome segregation and discrimination, many African Americans lost hope. Families became less stable. Crime increased. The 50-year nadir, not slavery, was the source of some of the bad social conditions that continue to plague black America today.

Legacies of the Nadir

Recent textbooks dipped their toes into the nadir but did not dive in. One of the books in my survey told how "African Americans found themselves forced into segregated neighborhoods." (Who did the forcing?) Several books told of lynchings, although none included a picture.

Textbooks should do a better job on this important period in our history. They would not have to start from scratch. African Americans have left a rich and bitter legacy from the nadir. To understand the plight of blacks as white America closed in on them, students could read Richard Wright's account of his childhood in *Black Boy* and Ida B. Wells's description of a lynching in *The Red Record.* They could sing aloud Big Bill Broonzy's "If You're Black, Get Back!" No book can communicate the depths of the black experience without including black voices.

Since the nadir, race relations have improved, due especially to the civil rights movement. But massive racial inequality remains. For example, in 2016 the median family income of African Americans was 61.5% of white family income. Wealth was even less equal. White families owned about ten times as much in property and investments. This is partly due to sundown suburbs that shut African Americans out of Veterans Administration and Federal Housing Administration home-ownership programs after World War II.

Money can be used to buy many things in our society. It can buy life itself, in the form of better health care and nutrition, as well as freedom from danger and stress. It's no surprise, then, that in 2015 African American men could expect to live four and a half years less, on average, than white men. Afri-

Thomas Shipp and Abram Smith had been arrested—but not yet stood trial—in Marion, Indiana, in 1930 when a mob pulled them from jail, beat them, and hanged them. Thousands of people witnessed the lynching. Some of the spectators appear in this photograph by Lawrence Beitler. Yet despite the public nature of the killings, no one was ever charged with the murders. This incident is a reminder that lynching occurred all over the nation, not just in the South.

can American women's life expectancy was five years less than white women's.

On average, African Americans still have worse housing, lower scores on IQ and SAT tests, and higher percentages of young men in jail. The sneaking suspicion that African Americans might be inferior lurks in the hearts of many whites and some blacks. It contributed to the modern revival of the KKK and to a backlash against schools' affirmative action policies, which some whites felt had given unfair advantages to people of color in college admissions. Ideas about racial inferiority also feed into the belief that black men who are brutally killed by police are somehow responsible for their own deaths. It is too easy to blame the victim and decide that people of color are responsible for being on the bottom. It is impossible to explain these differences without knowing about the nadir of race relations and the continuing influence of racism in U.S. history.

When textbooks make racism invisible in American history, they make it harder to see it in the present. Teachers say history is important because it gives us perspective on the present. If there is one issue in the present that should be related to the history our teachers and textbooks tell, it is racism. If white supremacy remains invisible in our textbooks and history courses, young people will have no tools to think intelligently about race relations in our future.

Chapter 6

JOHN BROWN, ABRAHAM LINCOLN, AND INVISIBLE IDEALISM

You may dispose of me very easily; I am nearly disposed of now. But this question is still to be settled—this Negro question, I mean; the end of that is not yet.

—JOHN BROWN

MORE THAN FIFTEEN YEARS BEFORE I WROTE THE first edition of this book, Frances FitzGerald studied an earlier generation of American history textbooks. In 1979 she published her findings under the title *America Revised*. A big problem with our textbooks, FitzGerald said, was that they left out ideas. As presented by the textbooks of the 1970s, "American political life was completely mindless."

Have things gotten better? Not really. Textbooks are full of facts and dates, but taking ideas seriously doesn't seem to fit their style. They tend to present events as if they unfolded by fate, along a line of steady progress. Including ideas would bring in uncertainty. It would mean looking behind the line of events to think about the ideas that caused them—and about the possibility that events could have gone a different way.

But textbooks don't like uncertainty. They present history without real drama or suspense, and without grappling with big ideas. Chapter 5 looked at racism, which lies behind much of our history but is rarely mentioned in our history books. This chapter looks at the opposite of racism, which is antiracism, or racial idealism. An ideal is the highest form of something, a standard to aim at. Antiracism's standard is complete racial equality. It is still not clear whether our society will live up to that ideal.

Our textbooks offer little help. Abolitionists and others who struggled against slavery in the nineteenth century could be role models for young people today and in the future. But just as our textbooks cover slavery without racism, they cover abolition without much idealism. Consider the case of John Brown, the most radical white abolitionist of all.

A passionate abolitionist, Brown (1800–1859) was deeply moved by the injustice and horror of enslavement. He considered it his Christian duty to help overthrow the institution, by taking up arms if necessary. When proslavery and antislavery forces clashed in Kansas, proslavery men violently attacked the antislavery town of Lawrence. Brown responded by leading antislavery volunteers in an attack on a settlement called Pottawatomie. They killed five proslavery men.

Brown's final and most famous act was leading an armed raid on a federal armory where military equipment was stored. The armory was located in Harpers Ferry, then in Virginia but now in West Virginia. Brown and his men managed to seize the armory. They hoped enslaved people would join the uprising, and some did, but the plan failed. The abolitionists were overcome by a mixed force of local volunteers and U.S. Marines, with deaths and injuries on both sides. Seven abolitionists were taken prisoner, including Brown. He was charged with murder, trying to start a slave rebellion, and treason against the state of Virginia. Brown was tried in Virginia, found guilty on all charges, and hanged.

Was John Brown Crazy?

The textbook treatment of Brown has changed over the years, like the treatment of slavery and Reconstruction. Before 1890, Brown was perfectly sane. Between 1890 and about 1970, he was insane. Since 1970 he has slowly been regaining his sanity.

When I set out to review six newer textbooks in 2006–7, I expected them to continue this trend. I thought they would show Brown's actions in a way that made them possible to understand. But I found that when it came to John Brown, these newer books were much the same as the twelve older books that dated back to the 1980s.

Brown himself didn't change after his death. (Well, he moldered a little more.) The changing picture of his mental health in our textbooks says more about the level of white racism in our society than about Brown. This might suggest that race relations in 2007 were not much better than in 1987.

In the eighteen textbooks in my survey, Brown was mentioned only in connection with Pottawatomie and Harpers Ferry. Authors did not write about his deep involvement with the abolition movement before Kansas. They did not share with students his thoughts or his arguments against slavery.

One particularly troublesome question is whether enslaved people supported Brown at Harpers Ferry. Six textbooks, including four of the newer ones, claimed that none joined him

Few Americans recognize the 1858 portrait of John Brown on the top. He looks like a middle-aged businessman, which he was. Later that year he grew a beard, partly to change his appearance after becoming wanted for helping eleven African Americans escape slavery in Missouri. But many Americans recognize the version below, painted on a wall of the Kansas State Capitol in 1937. It shows Brown as gaunt and deranged, followed by a tornado. Astoundingly, in the early 21st century, a textbook picked the 1937 version as its only image of Brown.

voluntarily. One said, "Brown and his party forcibly 'freed' about 30 slaves." It then drove home the point that the first person killed at Harpers Ferry was "an already-freed black gunned down by these 'liberators.'"

These accounts suggested that African Americans had no interest in freedom. This is bad history. Researchers have shown that Brown got considerable support from enslaved blacks around Harpers Ferry. They took an active part in the raid, and their resistance seems to have continued after it. One researcher noted that "the barns of all the jurors of John Brown's trial were burned—a time-honored signal of revolution."

Four textbooks were stuck in the days when Brown was considered to be a madman because of his actions. They described him as "almost certainly insane," or from a family with many insane members. His Harpers Ferry raid was called "a mad exploit." Not one author, old or new, showed any sympathy for Brown or any admiration for his ideals.

Brown's Idealism

I grew up reading that John Brown was at least fanatical, if not crazed. Textbook authors after 1890 called Brown mad because his actions made no sense to them. His plan was indeed far-fetched. Brown knew that. He told African American abolitionist Frederick Douglass that the raid would make a stunning impact on America even if it failed. He was right.

So what is the evidence for Brown's insanity? It's true that some of his lawyers and relatives wanted him to defend himself by claiming insanity. They were hoping to save him from hanging. But no one who knew Brown thought he was crazy.

"The Fanatical Figure"

Here is how a 2006 textbook titled *The American Pageant* described John Brown:

> *The fanatical figure of John Brown now stalked upon the Kansas battlefield. Spare, gray-bearded, and iron-willed, he was obsessively dedicated to the abolitionist cause. The power of his glittering gray eyes was such, so he claimed, that his stare could force a dog or cat to slink out of a room. Becoming involved in dubious dealings, including horse stealing, he moved to Kansas from Ohio with a part of his large family. Brooding over the recent attack on Lawrence, Old Brown . . . led a band of his followers to Pottawatomie Creek in May 1856. There they literally hacked to death five men, presumed to be proslaveryites. This fiendish butchery besmirched the free-soil cause and brought vicious retaliation from the proslavery forces.*

This language seems to come from the 1890–1940 nadir of race relations described in chapter 5, a time when most white Americans, including historians, felt that African Americans should not have equal rights. The original edition of this textbook came out way back in 1956, before the civil rights movement had a chance to affect our culture—or the writing of our textbooks.

Calling Brown a "fanatical figure" told students that he was unbalanced, if not actually insane. Why describe Brown as "stalking" upon the scene, instead of simply entering it? Other phrases, such as "dubious dealings" and "fiendish butchery," also paint a powerfully negative picture.

The negative slant also comes across in the choice of details to include and leave out. No reader of this account would guess that proslavery men had just killed five free-state settlers, including two in Lawrence. It is untrue that Brown moved to Kansas with his "large family."

In fact, some of his sons took their families to Kansas first and asked their father for aid after their proslavery neighbors threatened them. The account says the murdered men at Pottawatomie were "presumed" to be proslavery. They *were* proslavery. It also says that they were "hacked to pieces." They weren't.

Words have power, even when we are not aware of it. Part of being a good reader of history—in a textbook or anywhere else—is taking note of the words the author uses to paint a picture. See what effect they have on you. What extra layer of meaning are they adding, and why?

Brown made a good impression on people who spoke with him in jail, including his jailer and even reporters for proslavery Democratic newspapers. After a conversation with Brown, the governor of Virginia called him "a man of clear head" and said, "They are themselves mistaken who take him to be a madman."

Brown's words and his example had a big influence during the month between his trial and his execution, an impact that lasted long after his death. The fact that he talked about freeing the enslaved at once—an idea on the radical edge of abolitionist thought at the time—moved the national conversation about slavery a bit further in that direction.

As one of the biggest news stories of the day, Brown's trial and imprisonment were widely reported. People around the world were moved by his gracious behavior, speeches, and letters in the weeks before his death. His words made it clear that he viewed slavery as absolutely wrong, a violation of moral and Christian law. Brown objected that his death penalty was unjust, but he accepted it. He also took the opportunity to point to more serious injustices that were being carried out under the "enactments," or laws of the land:

Now, if it is deemed necessary that I should forfeit my life for the furtherance of the ends of justice, and mingle my blood further with the blood of my children and the blood of millions in this slave country whose rights are disregarded by wicked, cruel, and unjust enactments, I say, let it be done.

Brown's willingness to be hanged for what he thought was right had a moral force of its own. He was an idealist, but his idealism becomes invisible when his story gets taught in school. Twelve of the eighteen books I studied did not provide a phrase or even a word of what he wrote. Even Brown's jailer let him put pen to paper! But Brown's words, which moved a nation, cannot move students today.

It is easy simply to write off John Brown as insane. But it almost never helps us understand people who commit extreme, violent, or even repulsive acts—be they abortion clinic bombers, school shooters, or Middle Eastern hijackers—to label them mentally ill. It is harder to search for the causes of their actions. Doing so, however, might lead us to a bigger and more complex picture.

Blacks and Whites on Brown

Brown was controversial after his death. Many black leaders of the day, including Frederick Douglass and Harriet Tubman, knew and respected him. Douglass called Brown "one of the greatest heroes known to American fame." A black college deliberately chose to locate itself at Harpers Ferry. In 1918 its graduates put up a memorial stone to Brown: "That this nation might have a new birth of freedom, that slavery should be removed forever from American life, John Brown and his 21 men gave their lives."

His example impressed many white Northerners, too. As one "conservative Christian" put it in a letter Brown received in jail, "While I cannot approve of all your acts, I stand in awe of your position since your capture and dare not oppose you lest I be found fighting against God." Many people came to see Brown as a martyr who had sacrificed himself for a worthy cause. When the Civil War came, thousands of Americans made the same commitment to face death, partly in opposition to the system of enslavement. That's why Northern soldiers marched into battle singing "John Brown's Body," with its triumphant line, "His truth goes marching on."

Southern slave owners, on the other hand, were horrified by the sympathy Northerners showed to Brown. It made the owners of enslaved people determined to maintain slavery by any means necessary, including quitting the Union if Democrats lost the next presidential election.

Later, as the nineteenth century gave way to the twentieth, America entered its low point in race relations. African Americans lost their voting rights in the South, lynchings became common, and racism spread across the land, North as well as South. Now whites generally came to view Brown as insane.

It took the civil rights movement of the 1960s to free white America of enough of its racism to accept that a white person did not have to be crazy to die for black equality. Compare the 1961 textbook called *Rise of the American Nation* with its 1986 version, *Triumph of the American Nation*. The first one called the Harpers Ferry plan "a wild idea, certain to fail." The second one called it "a bold idea, but almost certain to fail." The difference is small but meaningful. John Brown has become a bit more sane. Even so, the textbooks still give no understanding of the role of antiracism in this or any other chapter of our past.

Abraham Lincoln: Racist or Antiracist?

Maybe textbook authors ignore John Brown's ideas because they feel his violent acts rule out any kind of sympathetic attention. But when we turn to Abraham Lincoln (1809–1865), one of the most honored figures in American history, we see that textbooks avoid his ideas, too.

Of course textbooks describe Lincoln with sympathy. Yet they also downplay his ideas, especially on the subject of race. Lincoln wrestled with the race question more openly than any other president, except perhaps Thomas Jefferson. But unlike Jefferson, Lincoln sometimes matched his actions to his words.

Lincoln recognized the basic humanity of African Americans early in his life. This may have been the influence of his father, who moved the family to Indiana partly because he disliked the racial slavery that prevailed in Kentucky. Or it may have come from a steamboat journey down the Ohio River in 1841, during which Lincoln was tormented by the sight of "ten or twelve slaves, shackled together with irons." Years later he wrote to the friend who had shared that trip with him that the memory of those people still had "the power of making me miserable."

As early as 1835, Lincoln served in the Illinois state legislature. There he cast one of only five votes against an antiabolitionist resolution. Textbooks often make it seem that the Republicans chose Lincoln as their presidential candidate in

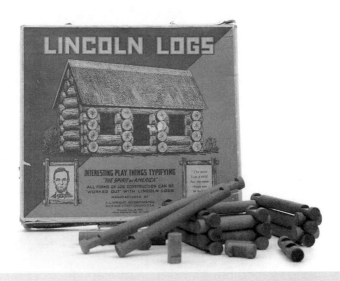

The log cabin in which Abraham Lincoln was born had a strange career that symbolizes what textbooks have done to Lincoln himself. The cabin fell into disrepair, probably before Lincoln became president. A hoax cabin was built in 1895. Later it traveled to Coney Island, New York, where it was mingled with another hoax: the birthplace cabin of Confederate president Jefferson Davis. Finally the "Lincoln cabin" was shrunk to fit inside a marble structure in Kentucky. The cabin also became a children's toy: Lincoln Logs, invented in 1920 by the son of famous architect Frank Lloyd Wright. The toy included instructions on how to build both Lincoln's cabin and Uncle Tom's cabin!

1860 because he was moderate, or held a middling position, on slavery. In fact, they chose him because of his "rock-solid antislavery beliefs." Two of the textbooks I reviewed quoted a letter from 1864 in which Lincoln wrote, "If slavery isn't wrong, then nothing is wrong."

Lincoln was antislavery, but he was not free of racism. It was possible to oppose slavery yet still doubt that black and white people could live together as equals. Although Lincoln ended segregation in the White House staff, he also asked his assistants

"To Save This Union"

Our history textbooks honor Lincoln mostly because he "saved the Union." By far their favorite statement of his comes from a letter he wrote to the *New-York Daily Tribune* on August 22, 1862, the second year of the Civil War. It appeared in fifteen of the eighteen books in my survey:

> *My paramount object in this struggle is to save the Union, and is not either to save or to destroy slavery. If I could save the Union without freeing any slave, I would do it; and if I could save it by freeing all the slaves, I would do it; and if I could save it by freeing some and leaving others alone, I would also do that.*

By emphasizing this quote, textbooks present a Lincoln who had no moral position on slavery and didn't care about black people. To present such a Lincoln, they have to omit two things about the quote.

First they leave out the very next point Lincoln made: that he has stated his goal according to his view of his *official* duty, but that he intends "no modification of my oft-expressed *personal* wish that all men, everywhere could be free." All but three of the textbooks left out this phrase, which makes clear his condemnation of slavery.

The other thing textbooks leave out is Lincoln's reason for writing. It was to seek support for the war from the people of New York City, one of the most Democratic (and white supremacist) cities in the North. Lincoln could never hope to win New York's support by claiming the war would end enslavement. He made the only appeal he could make: support the war and it will hold the nation together.

Not one author explained the political context of Lincoln's letter, or the audience it was meant for. None quoted Lincoln's words that same summer when he told a group of ministers "we shall need all the antislavery feeling in the country, and more." If they did, students would understand that Lincoln did have a moral position on the issue of slavery.

to look into the possibility of deporting African Americans to Africa or Latin America.

Most of our textbooks say nothing about Lincoln's wrestling with race. If they did, they would be splendid teaching tools! Young people would see that speakers emphasize different ideas to satisfy different audiences, so we cannot simply take their statements at face value. If textbooks recognized Lincoln's racism, students would learn that racism did not affect just extremists like Ku Klux Klan members. It has been "normal" throughout much of our history. And as they watched Lincoln struggle with himself to apply America's democratic principles across the color line, they would see how ideas can develop and a person can grow.

Lincoln's Idealism

Lincoln issued the Emancipation Proclamation on January 1, 1863. It freed enslaved people in the Confederacy and in some areas under U.S. control. But most textbook authors take pains to separate Lincoln from great idealism about slavery. They talk about the proclamation in terms of realpolitik, which views decisions as made for practical, political reasons.

One textbook I reviewed said that Lincoln "had reluctantly decided that a war fought at least partly to free the slaves would win European support and lessen the danger of foreign intervention on the side of the Confederacy." Political concerns did weigh on Lincoln, who was a master politician. But so did considerations of right and wrong. Textbooks don't allow for the possibility that Lincoln freed the enslaved at least partly because he thought it was right. It even hurt him politically—

Republicans lost control of Congress in November 1863, because many white Northerners would not favor black freedom for at least another year.

Abraham Lincoln was one of the great masters of the English language. Perhaps more than any other president, he used powerful symbols in speeches to move his audiences. Often they dealt with race relations and slavery. Consider his Second Inaugural Address, the speech he gave on March 4, 1865, when sworn in as president for the second time.

At the time, the Civil War was in its fourth bloody year. In this towering masterpiece of American speechmaking, Lincoln specifically identified differences over slavery as the main cause of the war:

> *If we shall suppose that American slavery is one of those offenses which, in the providence of God, must needs come, but which, having continued through his appointed time, he now wills to remove, and that he gives to both North and South this terrible war, as the woe due to those by whom the offense came, shall we discern therein any departure from those divine attributes which the believers in a living God always ascribe to him?*

Lincoln here suggests that the end of American slavery may be God's will and that the war may be God's punishment for slavery. He takes the idea further in his next long sentence, which draws a parallel between the suffering caused by the war and the suffering of "the bondman," or enslaved person:

> *Fondly do we hope—fervently do we pray—that this mighty scourge of war might speedily pass away. Yes, if God wills*

Black and white servicemen made up the crew of the USS Hunchback, a U.S. Navy gunboat during the Civil War. President Woodrow Wilson segregated the Navy, and racial integration further disappeared during the low point of race relations in the United States, between 1890 and 1940.

that it continue until all the wealth piled by the bondman's two hundred and fifty years of unrequited toil shall be sunk, and until every drop of blood drawn with the lash shall be paid by another drawn with the sword, as was said three thousand years ago, so still it must be said, "The judgments of the Lord are true and righteous altogether."

The Second Inaugural made a huge impact on Americans. A month later, after the president had been shot and killed, farmers in New York and Ohio greeted his funeral train with posters holding phrases from that speech.

When students today read that last long astonishing sentence aloud, they understand that it is a searing condemnation of America's sins against black people. Yet just one of the books in my survey included any of what I have quoted. Seven gave only the final phrase of the speech, about binding up the nation's wounds "with malice toward none." Ten ignored the Second Inaugural completely.

Lincoln's words tell us that he cared deeply about right and wrong. Moral considerations mattered in the Civil War. U.S. soldiers began fighting to save the Union. They ended by fighting for other ideas, too. They sang "The Battle Cry of Freedom," with the line "And although he may be poor, not a man shall be a slave." No one can sing that line today without seeing that the United States fought *both* to save the Union and to free the enslaved.

Challenging White Racism

It wasn't just Lincoln's antiracist idealism that challenged white racism during the Civil War. African Americans did so through their actions. After they were allowed to fight, their contributions made it harder for whites to deny that blacks were fully human. One Union captain wrote to his wife that although many whites consider "the entire Negro race" to be inferior, a few weeks of life with black troops would change their minds.

All eighteen of the textbooks in my survey at least mentioned that more than 180,000 African Americans served in the Union army and navy. A few included illustrations of black soldiers, and one mentioned that enslaved people helped Union soldiers who became trapped in Confederate territory. But only one book took the next step and pointed out that having black troops in Union forces led to a lowering of white racism.

The antiracism of the Civil War was especially powerful in the border states of Delaware, Maryland, Kentucky, and Missouri. Lincoln's Emancipation Proclamation had not affected slavery in these Unionist states—but the war did.

Maryland was a slave state that, at the beginning of the war, showed considerable support for the Confederacy. But it stayed with the Union and sent thousands of soldiers to defend Washington, DC. For Maryland whites to fight a war against slave owners while allowing slavery in their own state created tension. In 1864 Maryland abolitionists brought the issue of emancipation of the enslaved to a vote. Emancipation seemed to lose by a narrow margin—until the votes of absent soldiers and sailors were counted. Then it won by a large margin. The minds of these men had changed to favor freedom for African Americans.

As the war went on, Republicans campaigned on antiracism—and won. One New York Republican wrote, "The change of opinion on this slavery question . . . is a great and historic fact." People around the world supported the Union because of an idea: antiracism. Forty thousand Canadians, some of them black, came south to volunteer for the Union cause. As abolitionist senator Charles Sumner said, "Ideas are more important than battles."

Confusion in the Confederacy

White Southerners founded the Confederacy on the ideology, or idea system, of white supremacy. Historian Paul Escott has pointed out that throughout the Civil War, "the protection of

Throughout the nineteenth century, Harper's *magazine was the mouthpiece of the Republican or antislavery party. This 1864 illustration from the magazine takes words from the Democratic platform, that party's goals for governing. Thomas Nast's images highlight the shortcomings of the Democrats' plans. It is hard to imagine a political party today seeking white votes with such racial idealism.*

slavery . . . remained the central core of Confederate purpose." Textbooks downplay this idea, too, probably because they do not want to offend white Southerners today.

The racial ideas of the Confederacy did not help its war effort. It was part of the Confederate idea system that blacks liked slavery. The Confederate states, however, passed laws sparing some white men from military duty so they could oversee enslaved black people and keep them from revolting or running away. Throughout the war, Confederates kept as much as a third of their fighting force from the front lines. Instead, these

RESOLVED,—THAT IN THE FUTURE, AS IN THE PAST, WE WILL ADHERE WITH UNSWERVING FIDELITY TO THE UNION UNDER THE CONSTITUTION, AS THE ONLY SOLID FOUNDATION OF OUR STRENGTH

SECURITY, AND HAPPINESS AS A PEOPLE, AND AS A FRAMEWORK OF GOVERNMENT EQUALLY CONDUCIVE TO THE WELFARE AND PROSPERITY OF ALL THE STATES, BOTH NORTHERN AND SOUTHERN. RESOLVED,—THAT THIS CONVENTION DOES EXPLICITLY AMERICAN PEOPLE

The Democratic platform began innocently enough: "We will adhere with unswerving fidelity to the UNION under the CONSTITUTION as the ONLY solid foundation of our STRENGTH, SECURITY, and HAPPINESS as a PEOPLE." But Nast's illustration shows slave catchers and dogs chasing runaways into a swamp. It jolts the readers into asking, But what about them? These are people, too!

soldiers were scattered through areas with large enslaved populations, to prevent uprisings.

When the Union allowed Africans Americans to join the army and navy, Confederates' ideology made them claim it wouldn't work—blacks would hardly fight like white men. The undeniable bravery of the 54th Massachusetts and other black regiments proved them wrong. Later, when the South was reeling, Confederate president Davis suggested arming the enslaved to fight for the Confederacy. Their reward would be freedom.

Nast illustrated the Democrats' words "PUBLIC LIBERTY and PRIVATE RIGHT" with a riot that had taken place in New York in 1863. White thugs are exercising their "right" to beat and kill African Americans, including a child held upside down.

But supporters of slavery objected: if slavery was the best condition for blacks, how could freedom logically be a reward?

Black behavior proved that slaves *did* value freedom. Slavery broke down whenever Union armies came near. The flight of slaves toward Union forces brought ideological confusion to their former owners. Contradiction piled upon contradiction. Some Confederate leaders even said that to gain recognition from foreign countries, the Confederacy should give up slavery.

A month before the end of the war, the Confederate Congress finally passed a measure to enroll black troops. This showed that the war had raised slave owners' opinions of black abilities. It also showed complete disorder of ideas. What, after all, would these black soldiers be fighting *for*? Slavery? Secession? What would white Southerners be fighting for, once blacks were armed? As a Georgia owner said, "If slaves will make good soldiers our whole theory of slavery is wrong."

Some Confederate soldiers switched sides as early as 1862. When Union general William Tecumseh Sherman made his famous march through Georgia, his army got bigger because thousands of white Southerners joined it along the way. So did thousands of black Southerners. Meanwhile, almost two-thirds of the Confederate army that was fighting Sherman deserted. Confusion of ideas in the South, not just war-weariness, helps explain these facts.

The Union won the war partly because of the increasingly confused ideas in the South and the increasingly clear anti-racism in the North. Yet like Northern idealism, the white supremacist ideology of the South is largely missing from our histories. Our textbooks say little about ideas as a weakness of the South. They tend to present Union and Confederate sympathizers as equally idealistic. The North is shown as fighting to hold the Union together. The South, said one textbook in my survey, fought "for the preservation of their rights and freedom to decide for themselves." Decide *what* for themselves?

Nobody fought for racism in these accounts. Nobody fought to end it. The ideologies that divided our nation never come into clear view.

Reconstruction and Antiracism

After the Civil War, the nation entered the Reconstruction peri-od. But although the war had ended, conflict between the ide-ologies of racism and antiracism continued. Chapter 5 showed how the Southern states tried at first to resist change. They lim-ited the rights of newly freed African Americans with new laws based on the old rules of slavery. Northern voters reacted by electing strongly antiracist Republicans to Congress in 1866. Reconstruction entered a new, "radical" phase.

Antiracism became the policy of the nation. Congress passed the Fourteenth Amendment to the Constitution, making all persons citizens and guaranteeing them "equal protection of the laws." This shining jewel of our Constitution shows the idealism of the Republican Party at the time.

During Reconstruction a surprising variety of people went south to help the newly freed African Americans. Some were black Northerners. They knew all too well that not all white Southerners welcomed the new conditions. Edmonia Highgate, a black woman who had gone to Louisiana to teach school, reported that she had been shot at several times, and that some of her students had been "shot but none killed."

Other helpers were abolitionists who worked with African Americans to secure their civil and political rights. They oper-ated through the Freedman's Bureau, a government agency created for that purpose, or private organizations. Yet others who went south hoped to advance themselves by winning pub-lic office. The Northern white Republicans who lived in the South during Reconstruction were a diverse group, but nearly all the textbooks in my survey lumped them together under the

old term *carpetbaggers.* This term was created by white Southern Democrats as an insult. It suggested that those who came
south were the lowest dregs of Northern society, carrying all
their belongings in a type of cheap suitcase called a carpetbag,
swarming in to profit off the fallen South.

To insult white Southern Republicans, white Democrats in
the South used another term: *scalawag,* which means "scoun-
drel." Every Southern state had people who supported the United States. Some even joined the Union army. After the war,
most of these people became Republicans because they had
become convinced that equality was morally right. One of them
was a Mississippi planter named Robert Flournoy. He had led a
company of Confederate soldiers—until he gave up his post as
officer and returned home. He said, "[T]here was a conflict in
my conscience." During Reconstruction Flournoy helped orga-
nize the Republican Party in the South and published a newspaper called *Equal Rights.*

Some white Southerners joined the Republican Party
because it offered never-before-seen benefits, such as free public education for all. Others joined because they would rather
be on the winning side, or because they wanted to benefit from
ties with the new Republican state governments. The U.S. Congress had 113 white Republican members from Southern states
during Reconstruction. Fifty-three of them were born Southerners, many from wealthy families. White Southern Republicans,
then, were another diverse group. Yet again, nearly all textbooks
I looked at lumped them together under the old disgraceful term
"scalawags"—even if they suggested that "carpetbagger" was a
joke, or added that that not everyone used "scalawag."

Racial Idealists

Everyone who supported black rights in the South during Reconstruction ran a risk. At the beginning of the period, walking to school to teach could be life threatening. By the end of it, simply voting Republican was life threatening in some communities. These were dangerous ways to make a dollar. Not everyone was in Reconstruction for money. Racial idealism was the motive for most of the people who took the risk.

Textbooks deprive us of our racial idealists. None of the books I read, for example, mentioned Highgate or Flournoy. They treated Brown as a fanatic. They overlooked Lincoln's moral struggle and flattened his idealism to political decision making. When I ask my white college students on the first day of class to name their heroes in American history, only one or two in a hundred pick Lincoln, and none pick Brown. Yet these men, for all the complications of their thoughts and actions, were legitimate heroes of African Americans.

Antiracism is one of America's great gifts to the world. It led to "a new birth of freedom" after the Civil War, and not only for African Americans. The movement for black rights triggered the movement for women's rights. It has inspired people throughout the world. From South Africa to Northern Ireland, from East Germany to Vietnam and China, oppressed groups have borrowed methods and words from our abolition and civil rights movements. Yet we Americans seem to have lost these heroes. Teaching our history accurately would inspire us once again to value their idealism.

Chapter 7

THE LAND OF OPPORTUNITY

Ten men in our country could buy the whole world
and ten million can't buy enough to eat.

—WILL ROGERS

YOUNG PEOPLE HAVE EYES, EARS, AND MINDS. THANKS to the internet, social media, and popular culture such as movies and music videos, they also have a keen awareness of status, wealth, and privilege in America. They measure their own social position and that of their family and community against what they see. What do they learn from this?

"Why are people poor?" I have asked hundreds of first-year college students. Or, if they come from relatively privileged backgrounds, "Why is your family well-off?" Most of their answers are not well thought out and not well informed.

Students typically blame the poor for not being successful. They have no understanding of how social structure pushes people around, shaping both their ideas and their lives. Most do not realize that opportunity is not equal in United States. That is because we do a terrible job of teaching about social class,

This photo of a sweatshop—a crowded factory where people make clothing for low pay—in New York's Chinatown shows that workers still work under difficult conditions in the United States, just as they did a century ago, sometimes even in the same neighborhoods.

which includes money, background, status, education, privilege, and connections. Our textbooks echo a social archetype—that class does not exist in America, or if it does exist, it doesn't matter, because anyone can move up.

Is America All Middle Class?

The textbooks I reviewed barely mentioned social class, much less covered it in any meaningful way. Not one of them listed *social class, class structure, inequality, upper class,* or *lower class* in its index. Three of them listed *middle class*, but only to tell students that the United States is a middle-class country. Several of them talked about the growth of middle-class suburbs in the middle of the last century, after World War II.

The textbooks also failed to define what *middle class* means. Most definitions start with the median income. That amount changes over time, but it always means that half of all households earn more than the median income, and half earn less.

One easy way to define middle class is "households that earn between 75 and 125% of the median income." The proportion of middle-class households in the United States has steadily fallen since 1967. By about 1985, only 31% of households had incomes in that range. By 2011, the proportion had dropped to less than 21%.

After 1970, the middle class shrank during the presidencies of Ronald Reagan (1981–89), George H.W. Bush (1989–93), and George W. Bush (2001–9). Most families who left the middle class during those times went down, not up.

Only five of the eighteen textbooks I studied talked about separation by social class in America. Most of those dealt with the early colonies. They said things like this: "One great difference between colonial and European society was that the colonies had more social mobility."

Social mobility means moving from one class to another. Textbooks usually present this as the opportunity to move up. Our history also includes downward mobility and barriers to upward mobility, but these rarely appear in our textbooks. The reality, as sociologists have shown, is that most Americans die in the same class they were born into. Those who *are* mobile usually rise or fall just one class. Barriers to social mobility are higher in the United States than in other modern societies.

Rich and Poor

Social class is probably the single most important variable in society. From birth to death, it lines up with many other things we can measure. Pregnant women who are well-off are more likely than poor women to get good care during their pregnancies. Rich babies come into the world healthier and weighing more than poor ones.

When children from well-off families enter school, they are likely to go to schools that spend more on each student than the schools in inner cities or poor rural areas. Those same fortunate children are more likely than low-income children to live in households where they are exposed to books, music lessons, organized sports, summer camps, and other things that help them learn. It is no surprise that higher scores on the SATs—the tests that young people take before entering college—go along with higher social class. It continues through life. Social class matches up with whether or not people go to college, the kinds of jobs they get, how much money they earn, and whether they buy homes.

"From birth to death," I wrote in the first paragraph of this section. On average, death comes earlier to lower- and working-class people in the United States. The major reason is far better access to health care for those with money.

All kinds of events in our past can be seen as examples of social class at work. The right class can even buy life in the midst of danger. When the brand-new passenger ship *Titanic* sank in 1912, among the women and girls on board, only 4 of the 143 first-class passengers, who had paid most for the best quarters, were lost. Fifteen of 93 second-class passengers drowned, along

The Log Cabin Myth

Our system of government was created by rich men. Their ideas centered on government as a protector of people who owned property. One of the nation's founders and early presidents, James Madison, a rich man himself, worried about social inequality. He wrote a paper called *The Federalist No. 10* to explain how the government that was planned for the United States would not fall under the influence of the wealthy.

Madison's plan did not fully succeed. A historian named Edward Pessen studied the social-class backgrounds of all the American presidents through Reagan. He found that 40% of them came from the upper class, mostly from its upper fringes. Another 15% came from families between the upper and upper-middle classes. More than 25% came from upper-middle-class backgrounds.

A long-cherished belief in America is that anyone can rise to the highest office in the country from a humble background, whether it is a log cabin in the woods or a crumbling inner-city building. The reality is that, in Pessen's study, just six presidents, or 15%, came from the middle or lower-middle classes. Only one, Andrew Jackson, represented the lower class. It is no wonder that when Pessen published his research in 1984, he called his book *The Log Cabin Myth*. Since it came out, two presidents—Bill Clinton and Barack Obama—have come from working-class backgrounds. Donald Trump , who was president when this edition of *Lies My Teacher Told Me* was created, was a billionaire.

with 81 of 179 third-class women and girls. The crew ordered the third-class passengers to stay belowdecks during the emergency. They even held some back at gunpoint. Most men and boys, of whatever social class, perished. They had obeyed the lifeboat rule "women and children first."

During the 1960s and 1970s, all U.S. men of a certain age were subject to being drafted to fight in the Vietnam War. In spite of this "universal" draft, many sons of well-off families avoided being drafted. They were excused for medical reasons or because they were in college. Today's all-volunteer army relies even more on men and women from the lower class, who sign up as a way out of poverty. Textbooks and teachers ignore all this.

Hidden Injuries of Class

Some teachers avoid talking about social class because they don't want to embarrass any students. They should not worry. When my students from lower-income backgrounds learn about the class system, they feel liberated. Understanding the social processes that have helped keep their families poor helps them let go of feelings of shame about their status.

Understanding those same social processes helps kids from better-off backgrounds stop blaming victims for their own poverty. Students are fascinated to discover how the upper class has more than its fair share of power over everything from energy bills in Congress to zoning decisions in small towns.

More than any other racial or ethnic group, white working-class students believe that they deserve their low status. The result is a subculture of shame—one of what have been called "the hidden injuries of class." Two of my students provided a real-life demonstration.

The two drove around Burlington, Vermont, in a big, shiny, nearly new black luxury car. Then they drove the same route in a battered ten-year-old economy car. In each car, whenever they came to a red stoplight, they waited after it turned green until someone honked at them before they started driving. In the new luxury car, they waited almost twice as long before getting honked at. This experiment showed how Americans of all classes give respect to those they think are rich, educated, and successful.

Part of the problem is that we are taught that the United States is a meritocracy—that is, a society in which people advance based on their own merits, such as intelligence and skills, not on social class. However, a huge body of research proves that in fact education is dominated by the class structure and works to reinforce it. But when teachers and textbooks avoid talking about social class—as if it were a dirty little secret—working-class and lower-class families and students find it hard to talk about it.

American Inequality

Again and again, textbooks point out that the United States is less broken into social classes, and has more social mobility, than Europe. Here we see the social archetype of American exceptionalism at work again. This time, the message is "America is more fair than anywhere else." Does this prepare our young people for reality?

It certainly does not accurately describe our country today. Social scientists can measure inequality, which tells how evenly or unevenly wealth is spread within a society. One 2018 study used data from 2013–17 to compare income inequality in 38 industrial nations. The United States ranked seventh in income inequality, meaning that only six nations were more unequal. (South Africa was the least equal nation studied. Iceland was the most equal.)

So much for American inequality compared with other countries. What about over time? When did income inequality set in?

It is not a recent development. In 1910, the top 1% of the U.S. population received more than a third of all personal income. The bottom 20%, one-fifth of the population, got less than one-eighth of the total income. In 2016, according to the Federal Reserve Bank, the top 1% earned a somewhat smaller share, slightly less than a quarter of all personal income. But the top one-fifth of the population made just over half the total income, while the bottom one-fifth got a measly 3.1%.

Recently, income inequality has been getting worse. Consider chief executive officers, or CEOs, who are usually the highest-paid people in companies. In 1967, the average CEO in the United States made 26 times as much as the average worker. By 2004 the average CEO was making 431 times the average worker's pay.

Income is one thing. Wealth—which includes real estate and investments—is another. How does wealth inequality look in the United States? In 2017, the richest 1% of the households in the United States owned 40% of its wealth. The top one-fifth of households owned 90%, or nine-tenths, of the nation's wealth.

If textbooks covered inequality, they could describe how our class structure has changed over time. This could lead to a fascinating historical debate. Instead, it is another missed teaching opportunity.

Missing History

Why do textbooks and teachers steer clear of social class and income inequality? The main reason is that textbook publishers do not want to stir up the parents, committees that choose textbooks for school systems, and other watchdogs who see anything negative about the United States as unpatriotic. Discussion of class structure, especially, can be seen as unacceptable, even "socialist."

Another reason is heroification. Chapter 1 showed how this process keeps us from learning the full truth about historical figures such as Helen Keller and Woodrow Wilson. Textbook authors also tend to treat America itself as a hero, so they remove its warts.

Even reporting the facts about income and wealth might seem critical of America the hero. It is hard to come up with an idea of social justice that explains how 1% of us controls 40% of our national wealth. Could the other 99% of us really be *that* lazy or undeserving? Exploring some of the ways the upper class stays upper, such as through unequal education, would clearly involve criticism of our beloved nation.

More than math or science, more even than American literature, courses in American history hold the promise of telling young people how they, their families, their communities, and their society came to be as they are. Social class is one reason. History books and courses that leave it out are just one more way that education in the United States is rigged against the lower classes.

Chapter 8

KEEPING AN EYE ON THE GOVERNMENT

*What did you learn in school today, dear little boy of
  mine?*
I learned our government must be strong.
It's always right and never wrong. . . .
That's what I learned in school.

—Tom Paxton

MANY OF TODAY'S NEWER TEXTBOOKS ARE DOING
some things right. They have broadened their treatment of social
and cultural history. They give space to women, slavery, and
topics such as transportation and even popular music—things
that are part of our national story.

Even so, the focus of most textbooks remains the same as
it has traditionally been: the story of the United States government. What story have they told about it?

They certainly describe the government that was created
in 1789 and laid out in the Constitution. They talk about how
power was divided: some to the federal government, some to
the states, and some to individuals. They described the three

branches within the federal government that were created to balance each other, so that no one branch would gain too much power: the legislative branch (Congress), the executive branch (the president and Cabinet), and the judicial branch (federal courts, including the Supreme Court).

Every schoolchild learns about these branches and the famous "checks and balances" of our government. But textbook authors overlook the possibility that the Constitution's balance of powers has changed over the last 200 years. They also downplay the fact that many improvements in the environment, race relations, and education have been made not by government but by private citizens and nongovernmental groups.

Many textbooks, as a result, tell a story in which the government itself is the main actor on the stage of U.S. history. And not just an actor but a hero. Like other textbook heroes, this heroic state is pretty much without warts. But what do the textbooks say about some of the least heroic things our government has done? We'll look at how they handle two things: first, U.S. foreign policy, and second, the government's actions during the civil rights movement.

Three Views of the United States in the World

Chapter 1 talked about Woodrow Wilson's interference in other countries. That interference didn't stop with Wilson. But U.S. foreign policy is treated very differently in college courses on political science than it is in textbooks for high-school and younger students.

Some college professors and textbooks criticize what might

be called the American colossus. The reference is to the Colossus of Rhodes, a legendary statue of the ancient world that towered over the landscape. It gave us our word *colossal*, or "really big."

In this view, the United States has been the most powerful nation on earth since World War I, and it has acted to maintain its position of power. Critics of the American colossus say that we Americans long ago abandoned the ideals that inspired our Revolution, if we ever really held them. Now we prevent other nations and peoples from self-governing if we don't like their choices. We act like an empire, dominating lands around the globe.

A more common view at the college level is that U.S. foreign policy is based on realpolitik. This is politics based on facts and practical concerns rather than ideals and morals. In this view, America decides how to act abroad based solely on protecting its own interests. George Kennan, an official of the U.S. State Department, outlined realpolitik in a 1948 speech:

> We have about 50% of the world's wealth but only 6.3% of its population. In this situation, we cannot fail to be the object of envy and resentment. Our real test in the coming period is to devise a pattern of relationships which will permit us to maintain this position of disparity. We need not deceive ourselves that we can afford today the luxury of altruism and world benefaction—unreal objectives such as human rights, the raising of living standards, and democratization.

High-school American history texts do not show our country as a colossus trampling the rights of other countries. Nor do they do show the realpolitik view of the United States as coldly self-interested. Instead, they show a United States that

Textbook authors choose images to reinforce the idea that our country's main role in the world is to bring about good. Here a photograph from The Americans shows a Peace Corps volunteer in the African nation of Nigeria. I have no quarrel with the Peace Corps, but students should realize that its main impact has been on the development of its own volunteers, not on the other nations of the world.

acts in the world on behalf of human rights, democracy, and "the American way." When Americans have done wrong, it was because others misunderstood us, or maybe we misunderstood the situation. But always we meant to do good. We might call this the "international good guy" view of U.S. foreign policy.

Authors of high-school textbooks emphasize America's humanitarian side. And the United States does help other countries through foreign aid, although less than 1% of our national budget goes for that purpose. On the other hand, the United States stations troops in more than a hundred countries around the world. The United States also sponsors programs such as the Peace Corps, which sends young Americans to communities in developing nations to teach and help—although as one textbook in my survey pointed out, "Intelligent young Americans with high ideals seldom had enough of the knowledge or the skills required."

At least the Peace Corps means well. But another American influence abroad is more important and often less likable. That is our multinational corporations, large companies that are based in the United States but have business interests, including mining and manufacturing operations, in other countries. What role have these multinational corporations played in the affairs of other nations?

Big Business

In the 1970s, the American multinational company International Telephone and Telegraph (ITT) took the lead in getting the United States to undermine the government of Chile, in South America. Chile had elected a socialist president, Salvador Allende, and some in the United States felt that this was against U.S. interests. As a result, one company had a bigger effect on Chile than all the Peace Corps volunteers that the United States has ever sent to Latin America.

The same could be said of the Union Carbide Corporation in India, the United Fruit Company in Guatemala, and other U.S.-based companies in other nations. In some cases, multinationals have persuaded our government to get involved in other countries' affairs when only their corporate interest—not our national interest—was at stake.

All this matters a great deal to students, who may one day find themselves fighting in a foreign country partly because U.S. policy has been shaped by a corporation in Delaware, a bank in New York, or a construction company in Texas. Or young peo-

A Marine Corps General Speaks Out

Textbooks could use some of the realism shown by a former Marine Corps general named Smedley Butler. In 1931, looking back on his military career, Butler said:

> I helped make Mexico safe for American oil interests in 1914. I helped make Haiti and Cuba a decent place for the National City Bank boys to collect revenue in. I helped purify Nicaragua for the international banking house of Brown Brothers. . . . I brought light to the Dominican Republic for American sugar interests in 1916. I helped make Honduras "right" for American fruit companies in 1903. Looking back on it, I might have given Al Capone a few hints.

In case you don't know, Al Capone was a notorious American gangster.

ple's future jobs may disappear when multinationals move their factories or computer-programming centers to countries where people have to work for almost nothing.

When students try to understand the complex interweaving of politics and big business, they will get little help from their textbooks. Only three of the eighteen texts I examined even mention the word *multinational*. Textbooks should discuss how American multinational corporations act in other countries. They should also discuss how those corporations have influenced our own government.

Maybe they could start with the administration of Woodrow Wilson. Chapter 1 talked about how the United States interfered in Haiti and Russia during Wilson's presidency. Wilson got involved in Haiti partly because of pressure from the First National Bank of New York. Something similar happened in Russia. After the revolution introduced a communist state there, the Soviet government took over the country's oil-producing properties. This, according to historian Barry Weisberg, caused Standard Oil of New Jersey to become the major force behind the U.S. invasion of Russia in 1918.

Dark Deeds in Other Countries

The United States has performed some unsavory actions in other countries, including attempts to assassinate leaders and bring down governments. I looked at how all eighteen textbooks in my sample treated six U.S. attempts to undermine foreign governments.

1. Helping supporters of the shah of Iran overthrow Prime Minister Mossadegh and return the shah to the throne in 1953;

2. Helping bring down the elected government of Guatemala in 1954;

3. Rigging the 1957 election in Lebanon, which left the country's Christians in control and led to a Muslim revolt and civil war the next year;

4. Involvement in the assassination of Patrice Lumumba, leader of the African nation of Zaire (Congo) in 1961;

5. Repeated attempts to murder Fidel Castro, premier and later president of Cuba, and to bring down his government by terror, invasion, and sabotage;

6. Helping bring down the elected government of Chile in 1973.

When other countries do such things to us, we call it "state-sponsored terrorism." We would rightly be outraged to learn that another country, such as Cuba or Russia, had tried to influence our politics or undermine our economy. (Indeed, Russia's attempt to use the internet to affect our 2016 presidential election led to a major investigation, which was taking place while this book was completed in 2018.) So how did the textbooks talk about these U.S. activities in other countries?

In the case of Iran, the U.S. Central Intelligence Agency (CIA) arranged a coup that put the shah in full power in 1953. None of the original twelve textbooks mentioned this. However, all six of the newer textbooks mentioned our overthrow of Prime Minister Mossadegh. *The American Pageant* said this:

> *The government of Iran, supposedly influenced by the [Soviet Union], began to resist the power of the gigantic Western companies that controlled Iranian petroleum. In response, the . . . CIA helped engineer a coup in 1953 that installed the youthful shah of Iran, Mohammad Reza Pahlevi, as a kind of dictator. Though successful in the short run in securing Iranian oil for the West, the American intervention left a bitter legacy of resentment among many Iranians.*

These sentences do help young Americans to understand why in 1979 Iranians took over the American embassy in Iran, imprisoning the people inside for more than a year. They also explain Iran's continuing hostility to the United States and its policies in the Middle East.

Unfortunately, both newer and older textbooks did a bad job on the other five foreign adventures listed earlier. When they

On November 4, 1979, Iranian student activists stormed the U.S. Embassy in Iran's capital city to protest U.S. interference in Iranian politics. The students took 60 hostages and held them for 444 days.

did mention the events, they did not include America's sneaky actions. They said that the United States intervened "reluctantly" to control "chaos" or fight the spread of communism. Such shallow discussions did not help students who might want to know *why* "chaos erupted" or new conflicts followed our interventions. They definitely did nothing to help students explore possible connections between our interventions and other events.

The case of Cuba is especially interesting. Not one textbook mentioned our repeated attempts to assassinate Castro. According to testimony given to the U.S. Senate, the CIA had tried to kill Castro eight times by 1965. One was a botched attempt to get Castro to light an exploding cigar. Another was a contract with the criminal organization known as the Mafia to murder him. These and other efforts were dismal failures. Castro remained officially in charge of Cuba until 2008. He died at the age of 90 in 2016.

President John F. Kennedy ordered several ambitious attempts to bring down Castro and his government. Kennedy himself was assassinated in 1963. His accused killer, Lee Harvey Oswald, was killed before he could stand trial. Was Kennedy's assassination revenge for the attempts on Castro's life? Did Oswald act alone, as a government investigation decided, or was there a possible Cuban or Mafia connection?

Because textbooks don't mention Kennedy's attempts to have Castro killed, they cannot explore those possible connections. The authors stick with vague statements like this one: "Some investigations support the theory that Oswald was involved in a larger conspiracy, and that he was killed in order to protect others who had helped plan Kennedy's murder."

What Should We Say About Skullduggery?

Should textbooks include all government skullduggery? Certainly not. Just as we cannot mention every good or positive moment in our history, we should not look relentlessly at the darker moments. But textbooks should analyze at least *some* of our foreign interventions in depth. They raise important issues.

One issue is our reason for interfering in other countries. It is hard to defend hidden, secret violence as being moral or "the right thing to do." Or maybe our interventions make sense in terms of realpolitik. Perhaps secret attacks on other countries and their leaders *are* practical ways to deal with international problems.

But the six cloak-and-dagger operations listed in this chapter either failed to solve problems or created bigger problems at a later date. The CIA's attempts to bring down Castro not only failed, but may have made him more popular in Cuba. Even when the operations succeeded in the short term, as in Iran, they undermined America's long-term interest. They tarnished the United States by linking it with illegal actions and undemocratic governments.

Another issue is secrecy. All six of the interventions I listed were covert, meaning that they were hidden from the public. Does such secrecy belong in a democracy?

Our democracy relies on openness. A covert violent operation against a foreign nation, political party, or individual violates that openness. It also leads to lying to the American people. Citizens of the United States cannot possibly debate or criticize government policies or actions if they don't know about them. Yet the U.S. government covered up all six of the operations on my list—and many more—and lied about most of them. When the truth does come out, "national security" is usually given as the reason for the secrecy.

One president caught in a lie was Dwight D. Eisenhower. During the Cold War, the Soviets accused the United States of flying spy planes over their country. Eisenhower denied it—only to have a captured American pilot named Francis Gary Powers admit the truth on Russian television. The Soviets had shot down his CIA spy plane over Russia.

Much later, the public learned that Powers had been just the tip of the iceberg. During the 1950s, at least 31 U.S. flights were shot down over Russia, with more than 170 Americans aboard. For decades our government lied to the families of the lost men and never tried to have their bodies returned, because the flights were illegal and were supposed to be secret.

Covert operations are always undertaken by the executive branch of government, presidents and their advisors. Often they keep actions covert because they suspect the actions would not be popular with Congress or with the American people. Textbooks cannot report accurately on any of the six foreign operations listed in this chapter without mentioning that the U.S. government covered them up. The textbooks' "international good guy" approach is a failure if we want citizens who can think clearly about American foreign policy.

The Full Story of the Civil Rights Movement

Just as they do with U.S. foreign policies, college courses differ from textbooks for younger students on U.S. domestic policies—the decisions and actions that the government takes *inside* the United States. College courses study the many forces that shape domestic policy. Many lower-level textbooks simply give the government credit for most of what gets done. It is especially upsetting to watch this happen to the story of the civil rights movement, where the courageous acts of thousands of citizens in the 1960s begged and even forced the government to act.

Between 1960 and 1968, the civil rights movement repeatedly asked the federal government for protection. It also asked it to enforce the Fourteenth Amendment to the Constitution, which defines citizenship and bans any state from limiting the rights of any citizen, and related laws that were passed during Reconstruction.

The government's response was woefully weak. How the Federal Bureau of Investigation (FBI) answered the movement's call was particularly important, because the FBI is the leading national law-enforcement agency. Unfortunately, the FBI had a history of hostility toward African Americans.

In its early years, the FBI had a few black agents. By the 1930s, director J. Edgar Hoover had weeded out all but two. By the 1960s the FBI had not one black agent (although Hoover tried to claim it did, by counting his two chauffeurs). The bureau had few agents in the South. Many of those it did have there were white supremacists. In Mississippi it had no office at all. There the bureau got its information from local sheriffs and police chiefs—often the very people from whom the civil rights movement wanted to be protected.

Hoover was an open white supremacist. In 1963 he launched a campaign to destroy Martin Luther King Jr. and the civil rights movement in which King had become a leader. With the approval of Robert Kennedy, the attorney general of the United States, Hoover's FBI tapped King's phones, bugged his hotel rooms, and recorded his private conversations. Some of these secret recordings involved King's relations with women other than his wife. The FBI gave them to members of the government, reporters, and others. It sent one of the tape recordings to the office of King's organization, the Southern Christian Leadership Council (SCLC), with a note suggesting King kill himself.

The bureau hoped to blackmail King into leaving the civil rights movement, or to embarrass him and cause his wife to divorce him. Neither of those things happened, but the FBI carried on harassing King and trying to undermine him. It also refused to share with King information it received about death threats to him. The bureau knew these threats were serious. Civil rights workers were being killed. The FBI repeatedly claimed that protecting civil rights workers from violence was not its job.

The Movement Takes Action

In 1962 a civil rights group called the Student Nonviolent Coordinating Committee (SNCC, pronounced "snick") sued Robert Kennedy and J. Edgar Hoover to get them to protect civil rights workers. Two years later the civil rights movement organized "Freedom Summer" to bring hundreds of Northern students, mostly white, to Mississippi to work among African Americans for civil rights. That summer, white supremacists bombed 30 homes and burned 37 black churches across the state. After three civil rights workers were murdered, a national outcry led the FBI to open a Mississippi office at last.

The FBI attacked black and interracial organizations across the South and across the nation. In 1964, after Congress passed the Civil Rights Act, students from a black college protested when a bowling alley in Orangeburg, South Carolina, refused to obey the law. State troopers fired on the protestors, killing three. Twenty-eight others were wounded. Many were shot in the bottoms of their feet as they threw themselves on the ground to avoid the gunfire. The FBI not only did not help identify the officers who had fired, it provided false information about the students to help the officers defend themselves in court.

In 1970, Hoover approved FBI investigation of "all black student unions and similar organizations organized to project the demands of black students." Tougaloo College in Mississippi, where I taught, was a special target. At one point, FBI agents in Jackson even proposed to "neutralize" the entire college, in part because students had sponsored "out-of-state Negro speakers, voter-registration drives, and African cultural seminars and

Starting in 1961, activists called Freedom Riders traveled by bus through the South to protest racial segregation and the failure of local authorities to enforce laws against it. The Freedom Riders endured arrest, imprisonment, and beatings but succeeded in drawing attention to their cause.

lectures . . . [and] condemned various publicized injustices to the civil rights of Negroes in Mississippi." Such crimes!

The list of FBI wrongdoing in connection with civil rights is long. It is even possible that the FBI or CIA was involved in the murder of King in 1968. Certainly the FBI has never shown any interest in uncovering the conspiracy that killed King. It even tried to prevent his birthday from becoming a national holiday.

The FBI's actions—and the federal leadership that allowed them and sometimes asked for them—are part of the legacy of the 1960s. Like the positive achievements of that period, such as the Civil Rights Act of 1964 and the Voting Rights Act of 1965, the government's attack on the civil rights movement is part of our history. Many textbooks, however, have simply left out anything bad the government did.

Such textbooks didn't just fail to tell how the federal government had worked against the civil rights movement. Many of them credited the government for almost single-handedly bringing about the positive achievements of the period. They left too many young African Americans thinking that desegregation—passing laws against separating people by race—was something the government did from the top down. They had no idea that it was something the black community forced on the government from the bottom up.

Fortunately, textbooks have improved in their treatment of the civil rights movement. All six of the newer texts I examined told how police attacked African Americans in Selma, Alabama, when they tried to vote. All six told how a 50-mile protest march in Alabama, led by King, prodded President Lyndon B. Johnson and Congress to pass the Voting Rights Act.

These and some other textbooks show how the civil rights movement worked. African Americans, often with white allies, nonviolently challenged an unjust law or practice. This led whites to violently "defend civilization." This violence, in turn, horrified enough people across the land to bring about changes to the law or practice. The civil rights victories of the 1960s came about not because the government thought it was a good idea, but because of the courage of civil rights volunteers.

Truth and Citizenship

Textbook authors seem to believe that Americans can be loyal to their government only if they believe it has never done anything bad. They present a U.S. government that deserves students' loyalty, not their criticism.

One textbook reviewer wrote, "We live in the greatest country in the world. Any book billing itself as a story of this country should certainly get that heritage and pride across." He reviewed a text that described the basic forces and events of the civil rights movement. That book gave the impression that the U.S. government was not doing all it should for civil rights. Perhaps that's why the reviewer declared that that particular book should not be used.

Textbooks that present only admiring accounts of the government may get chosen for use in schools, but they don't win students' attention. Young people are smart enough to question what they are told, especially if seems one-sided and too good to be true. Students who learn little or nothing in school about the bad things their government has done, especially when the media and sometimes their parents tell a different story, do not end up thinking their government is perfect. Instead, they become suspicious of education.

Most adult Americans no longer trust the government without question, as they had in the 1950s. Since that time, many cases of misconduct and lying by the executive branch of the federal government have come to light. They have shattered the trust of the American people. In 1964, 64% of Americans still trusted the government to "do the right thing." Thirty years later, only 19% of them did.

Textbooks—and all of us—need to understand the difference between patriotism and nationalism, which is an extreme kind of patriotism in which people feel that their country is superior to all others, and that its interests override everyone else's. African American abolitionist Frederick Douglass said that patriots hold their country accountable for its sins and do not excuse them. A nationalist, on the other hand, denies that the country ever committed sins and cannot think rationally about them.

By taking a nationalist approach to the federal government, downplaying its secret and illegal acts, textbooks discourage young people from thinking about important issues, such as how the executive branch uses power. By presenting government actions without the pressures that caused them—whether from multinational corporations or civil rights organizations—textbooks miss the chance to show how the people and their leaders make history together.

Nationalist history doesn't really work. Surely we need education that helps young people critique their government intelligently. Nationalistic education is not want we want. Indeed, nationalism is not patriotic.

Chapter 9

SEEING
NO EVIL
IN VIETNAM

*Without censorship, things can get terribly
confused in the public mind.*

—GENERAL WILLIAM WESTMORELAND

AS WE COLLEGE PROFESSORS GROW OLDER, WE GET more and more astonished by what our students don't know about the recent past. As the 1970s became the 1980s, I saw this happen to the Vietnam War. When I lectured on it I got increasingly blank looks—even though U.S. troops had fought in Vietnam until 1973, and Vietnam had sparked the biggest antiwar protest movement in American history.

In 1987 I gave my students a quiz that included the question "Who fought in the war in Vietnam?" Almost one-fourth of the students answered, "North and South Korea." I was stunned! This was like asking "When did the War of 1812 start?" and getting the answer "1957." In fact, people who graduated from high school in the 1980s and 1990s might have known more about the War of 1812 than about the Vietnam War.

It's not the students' fault. The original twelve textbooks I reviewed devoted the same coverage—nine pages—to each war.

Yet the War of 1812 took place long ago, lasted half as long as the Vietnam War, and killed maybe 2,000 Americans, compared with 58,000 U.S. deaths in Vietnam.

Was the War of 1812 so important that it deserved equal space? The textbooks did not say so. Most of their authors claimed no special importance for the War of 1812. They used the space to give plenty of details about individual heroes and battles in that war. One book spent three paragraphs on the naval Battle of Put-in-Bay in Lake Erie. That works out to one paragraph for each hour of battle. Vietnam got no such coverage. To this day, however, our country feels the lingering effects of the Vietnam War.

A Quick Look Back

The Vietnam War arose because in the 1880s France held part of Southeast Asia—including Vietnam—as a colony. During World War II, Japan took over. At the end of the war, communists and nationalists across Vietnam rose up and declared their country's independence under Ho Chi Minh. (Decades earlier, a young Ho had pleaded with Woodrow Wilson to help Vietnam gain self-determination, as mentioned in chapter 1.)

Neither France nor the United States recognized the claim. France tried to restore its colonial rule. The United States sent military advisors to help the French.

In 1954, France withdrew from Vietnam after a crushing defeat in battle. A treaty divided Vietnam into two temporary zones. North Vietnam was communist, led by Ho Chi Minh. The United States propped up the newly formed government and army of South Vietnam. The country was supposed to hold nationwide elections in 1956, but the dictator of South Vietnam blocked them, knowing that Ho Chi Minh would win.

The country was in turmoil. Refugees from communism poured south. At the same time, South Vietnam proceeded to attack its own people, especially those who disagreed with or opposed the government. This repression by the government led to armed resistance in South Vietnam, supported by the government of North Vietnam.

By 1962, there were 11,000 American military advisors in South Vietnam. Two years later, North Vietnam fired at a U.S. ship in the Gulf of Tonkin, off the coast of Vietnam. President Lyndon B. Johnson falsely claimed a second attack on the ship, and Congress authorized war in August 1964.

Fighting raged for years, and the war became steadily more unpopular in the United States. In 1973, the last American troops left Vietnam. Two years later, North Vietnamese troops marched into Saigon, the capital of South Vietnam. They had won control of the now reunified country.

Images of War

Photographs have recorded American wars since Matthew Brady took a camera to his first Civil War battlefield. The Vietnam War was especially visual. It is still our most televised and photographed war.

I focused my textbook review on images, thinking that would be more impartial than criticizing authors for wrong interpretations of the war. After all, someone could argue that *my* interpretation was wrong. During the Vietnam War, photographers released a stream of images that seared themselves into the

Nguyen Ngoc Loan, the national police chief of South Vietnam, casually shot a member of the Viet Cong on a Saigon street in 1968, as an American photographer and television crew looked on. This photograph helped persuade many people in the United States that their side in the Vietnam War was not morally superior to the communists'.

minds of people around the world. Five of the best-known images of the war were:

1. A Buddhist monk sitting on a street in Saigon, burning himself to death to protest the South Vietnamese government;
2. A little girl crying as she runs down a highway after South Vietnamese airplanes accidentally dropped the chemical weapon napalm on her village;
3. The national police chief of South Vietnam shooting a member of the Viet Cong, the communist South Vietnamese rebels, through the head;
4. Bodies lying in a ditch after U.S. troops killed them in a village named My Lai; and

5. Americans leaving a Saigon rooftop by helicopter, ahead of the arrival of North Vietnamese troops, as desperate South Vietnamese try to climb aboard.

What use did textbooks make of these images, some of which were published thousands of times and became famous in their own right?

In 1995 the twelve textbooks in my original sample failed miserably. One book included the photo of the police chief executing the terrified man. No other textbook used any of them.

Of the six newer books I reviewed for the second edition of *Lies*, three provided much more coverage of the Vietnam War. One of them gave the war 21 pictures and more than 34 pages. Still, only one of those pictures—the burning monk—came from my list of the war's most powerful images. None of them showed any damage that the United States did to Vietnam. Another book included both the burning monk and the rooftop flight, and a third had the rooftop flight. That was it. The other three had none of the photographs.

The makers of textbooks can choose from thousands of images of the Vietnam War. They could have selected photos not on my list and still done justice to the war. But at the very least, textbooks should show the violence we did to Vietnamese citizens. This was a war in which our armed forces had only a foggy notion as to who was an enemy and who was an ally. Attacking civilians was actually U.S. policy. As General William Westmoreland said, "It does deprive the enemy of the population, doesn't it?"

The fourth photograph on my list did not appear in any of the textbooks I examined. It came out of an infamous attack on civilians—the My Lai massacre.

The Importance of My Lai

The My Lai massacre took place in March 1968, when U.S. troops shot and killed 400 women, children, and old men in a South Vietnamese village. The officer in charge of the raid was tried in military court and sentenced to life in prison, but his sentence was reduced. He served only three and a half years under house arrest.

My Lai is important for several reasons. It is a symbol of the violence suffered by the Vietnamese people during the war.

American troops murdered women, old men, and children in the My Lai massacre. Ronald Haeberle's photographs, including this one, which ran in Life magazine, seared the massacre into the awareness of the United States. Most Hollywood movies about Vietnam include My Lai imagery. Platoon is a vivid example.

On April 29, 1975, this helicopter evacuated people from a Saigon rooftop. Saigon fell to the communists the next day, ending the long American (and Vietnamese) nightmare.

Vietnam veteran John Kerry, who became a U.S. senator, said that actions such as My Lai were "not isolated incidents but crimes committed on a day-to-day basis with the full awareness of officers at all levels of command."

Only one textbook I surveyed—the oldest one—treated My Lai as anything other than an isolated incident. One of the newer books had a good paragraph about My Lai, but it never mentioned that attacks on civilians were a general problem. The rest said even less or never mentioned My Lai at all. Silence on this subject leaves students ignorant about an important feature of the war.

It also leaves them unable to fully understand the antiwar movement. The movement was driven in part by Americans' growing awareness of violence like that at My Lai. Much of that

President Lyndon B. Johnson visited U.S. troops at a base in Cam Ranh Bay during the war. This is the only picture of troops that appears in one of the textbooks I surveyed.

awareness came from photographs and footage seen on television news. When *Life* magazine published photographer Ronald Haeberle's picture of the bodies of the My Lai victims, the image instantly became one of the most disturbing and memorable scenes to come out of the war. Images of the war did not just record history, they *made* history. They changed the way people around the world understood the conflict.

Teaching Vietnam

If textbooks left out the important photographs of the Vietnam War, what images *did* they include? For the most part, they used uncontroversial pictures, such as soldiers walking through rice

Too Difficult for You?

My list of important Vietnam photographs had five images. You'll notice that only three of them appear in this chapter. What about the other two?

Textbook authors and publishers are extremely nervous about showing anything that might upset anyone—not necessarily students, but teachers, parents, or people in the community. For that reason, one of the most famous photographs of the Vietnam War was absent from every textbook I reviewed for *Lies My Teacher Told Me,* and another appeared only once. They were most likely left out because they show death, suffering, and, in one case, nudity.

Quang Duc was a Buddhist monk who set himself on fire to protest the South Vietnamese government that the United States supported. The photograph of him sitting unmoving in the middle of a city intersection, wrapped in flames, watched by other monks and citizens, shocked both the South Vietnamese and the American people. Before the war ended, several other Vietnamese and at least one American followed Quang Duc's example.

Kim Phuc was nine years old when napalm, a highly flammable sticky gel, was dropped on her village. Her clothes caught fire. She stripped off the burning garments and ran, screaming and crying, down a highway with other terrified villagers. She survived, but the photo of her agony was one of the most searing images of the war. One of my students wrote to me, "To show a photograph of one naked girl crying after she has been napalmed changes the entire meaning of that war to a high school student."

I left these two photographs out of this young readers' version of *Lies My Teacher Told Me* for a simple reason. They might have prevented you from getting the book in your school library, or using it in a classroom. That's because some adults think children are not mature enough to handle such images. I don't agree, but what do you think?

paddies or jumping out of helicopters. Ten of them showed damage caused by the *other* side.

The textbooks left out other things, too. After a major attack, one U.S. army officer involved in recapturing a village said, "It became necessary to destroy the village in order to save it." For millions of Americans, that statement summed up what the United States did in Vietnam. Not one of the eighteen textbooks included it. Most books also left out the songs and chants of the antiwar protestors who marched in American streets. Above all, textbooks failed to capture the surging, conflicting emotions of the time.

Three of the newer textbooks did better than the rest. They gave more space to the antiwar movement and to the dirty underside of the war. That may be due to the passage of time. As the Vietnam War moved further into the past, authors of new textbooks may have felt free to start treating it more fully and honestly, as some new books now treat slavery.

How should Vietnam be taught? I don't want to fault textbook authors for interpreting the issues of the war differently than I do, but it seems that any reasonable treatment would cover at least these questions:

Why did the United States fight in Vietnam? What was the war like before the United States entered it? How did the United States change the war? How did the war change the United States? Why did an antiwar movement become so strong? What were the movement's criticisms of the war? Were they right? Why did the United States lose the war? What lessons should we take from the war?

I shall discuss only the first question here—but if you study the Vietnam War, in school or on your own, you may want to search out answers to the other questions.

So why *did* the United States fight in Vietnam? The "international good guy" view that I described in the last chapter would say that we fought to bring democracy to the Vietnamese people. A view based on realpolitik, also described in the last chapter, is the "domino theory." Some of our leaders believed that if Vietnam "fell" to communism, so would other nations in Southeast Asia, as a row of dominoes falls after the first one is knocked down.

Some historians see our involvement in Vietnam as part of a long history of racism and empire building that started with the first Indian war in Virginia in 1622. Connected with this view is America as a "colossus." In this interpretation, the leaders of the United States worried that our standing in the world was on the line. A defeat in Vietnam would make the United States look weak and threaten its ability to dominate other parts of the world. Also related to this thinking is an important domestic political consideration: no president wanted to be seen as the one who "lost" Vietnam, so they went on supporting the war.

Some conspiracy theorists go further. They claim that big business encouraged the war in order to boost the U.S. economy, or that Vietnam had important rubber, oil, or mineral resources that we needed.

A final view might be that there was no clear cause or purpose for our involvement in Vietnam. In this view, we blundered into the war because in 1946 we made the mistake of taking a stand against the independence movement that was popular in Vietnam, and no presidential administration afterward had the courage to undo that mistake. Perhaps the seeds of our tragic involvement were planted as early as 1918, when Woodrow Wilson refused to hear Ho Chi Minh's plea for his country's independence. But textbooks rarely suggest that the events of one period in history cause events in the next period. I was not surprised that none of the textbooks I surveyed looked before the 1950s to explain the Vietnam War.

Historical evidence for some of these conflicting interpretations of the war is stronger than for others. But textbooks need not choose sides. They could present several interpretations, with an overview of the evidence for each one, and invite students to come to their own conclusions. We have seen, however, that textbook authors seem driven to provide a "right" answer, even when historians are still debating a controversy.

Dodging the Issue

Instead of choosing any interpretation of the cause of our war in Vietnam, most textbooks simply dodge the issue. Here is what one text in my survey said: "Later in the 1950s, war broke out in South Vietnam. This time the United States gave aid to the South Vietnamese government."

War broke out. What could be simpler? The same textbook that spent four pages discussing why the United States got into the War of 1812 spent just these two sentences on why we fought in Vietnam.

The texts I examined did nothing to help students think critically about the Vietnam War and support their conclusions with evidence. Never did they raise questions like "Was the war right?"

Some books appear to raise moral questions, but then veer away. One of them, for example, asked, "Why did the United States use so much military power in South Vietnam?" Trying to answer that question could get interesting. Was it because our enemy wasn't white? Because the enemy couldn't strike back at the United States? Simply because we had the military force available to use? Was it because the United States has a history of conquering peoples we see as "primitive"? Because the United States is like most nations and acts not out of morality but out of realpolitik? If so, how *was* this war in our national interest?

The teacher's edition of this textbook provides the answer that the authors are looking for. It shows that they don't really want students to think about *any* of these possibilities. It simply parrots President Johnson's excuse for the heavy bombing: "To show the Viet Cong and their ally, North Vietnam, that they could not win the war." This answer is mystifying, because the Viet Cong and North Vietnam *did* win the war.

All but one of the high-school textbooks I examined shied away from actually prompting students to think critically about the Vietnam War. The one exception had been published in 1974, the year after the last U.S. troops withdrew from the war.

By 1986, at least 70% of Americans considered the war to have been morally wrong. But Vietnam can still be controversial. That may be why the American Adventure exhibit at Disney World left the Vietnam War completely out of its 29-minute history of the United States. That may explain why the Smithsonian Institution awkwardly shoehorned its treatment of the war into the heading "The Price of Freedom." And it may explain why even the newer history textbooks I reviewed left out the images and issues that might trouble students—or their parents—today.

Mystifying the Vietnam War left students unable to understand many public debates since then. Politicians often speak of "the lessons of Vietnam" when talking about military interventions in other countries, most recently Iraq. Our textbooks do not help young people understand what those lessons are supposed to have been.

Vietnam has also come up in discussions of secrecy, the press, how the federal government operates, and even whether the military should admit gays. Young people have a right to enough knowledge about Vietnam to take part intelligently in these debates. After all, they are the people who will be called on to fight our next war.

Chapter 10

THE DISAPPEARANCE OF THE RECENT PAST

*When information which properly belongs to the people
is systematically withheld by those in power, the people
soon become ignorant of their own affairs, distrustful of
those who manage them, and—eventually—incapable
of determining their own destinies.*

—RICHARD M. NIXON

SOME EASTERN AND CENTRAL AFRICAN SOCIETIES
divide the dead and the past into what are called *sasha* and
zamani in Kiswahili. The sasha, or living-dead, are those who
died recently. Their lives overlapped with those of people who
are still here. They are not wholly dead because they still live in
the memories of the living.

When the last person to know an ancestor dies, the ancestor
leaves the sasha for the zamani. The zamani are the dead who
are not remembered as living people by anyone still alive. They
are not forgotten—they are honored as ancestors. But they are
no longer living-dead.

We may not use these African terms, but we divide our

past in a similar way. Our sasha is the past that we have lived through—or if not us, then people who are still alive in the world lived through it. Our zamani is the more distant past. It is known not through living memories but through other sources, such as documents and photographs.

Authors of American history textbooks treat the sasha and the zamani very differently. They seem comfortable in the zamani. They honor our cultural ancestors—such as George Washington or Clara Barton, founder of the American Red Cross—who are safely in the distant past.

The world of the sasha is controversial. Readers bring to it their own memories, knowledge, and understanding. If they are young, they may compare what they are taught in school with what they have heard from older people in their lives. Either way, the views of the living may not always agree with what is written. Therefore, the less said about the recent past, the better.

Tiptoeing Through the Sasha

For the first edition of *Lies* I wanted to see how textbooks dealt with the recent past. I examined ten of the books in my original sample, and I defined *recent past* as "the five decades before the 1980s." (Several of the books came out in the 1980s. They could not be expected to cover that decade fully.)

On average, the textbooks gave 47 pages to the 1930s, 44 pages to the 1940s, and fewer than 35 pages to the 1950s, 1960s, and 1970s. Even the turbulent decade of the 1960s—with the civil rights movement, most of the Vietnam War, and the assassinations of Medgar Evers, Martin Luther King Jr., President

John F. Kennedy, and his brother, Attorney General Robert Kennedy—got fewer than 35 pages.

Textbooks in 2006–7 were quite different. The books I reviewed for the second edition of *Lies* gave the 1960s an average of 55 pages, more than any other decade of the twentieth century. That's because the 1960s had moved further into the past and no longer felt "recent."

But the newer texts had their own recent past—the 1980s and 1990s. They devoted fewer than twenty pages each to these decades, even including the first few years of the 21st century. Yet these were decades in which the United States twice attacked Iraq, had a close and hotly argued presidential election (between George W. Bush and Al Gore) that went to the Supreme Court, and endured a terrorist attack on 9/11/2001. In contrast, the newer batch of books gave an average of 49 pages to the 1930s and 47 to the 1940s—much more than the older books had given to those decades!

Many events of the 1980s and 1990s were still controversial when the newer batch of textbooks were written. One example is the 1998–99 impeachment and trial of Bill Clinton, a Democratic president. Some students' parents are Republicans, and some are Democrats, so what textbook authors might say about Clinton could offend half of the community. Textbook authors tiptoe through the sasha with extreme caution, trying to avoid upsetting anyone.

Textbooks are not the only reason that history classrooms shortchange the recent past. Teachers, too, may approach the events and issues of the recent past with caution, or even nervousness. Often there simply isn't time. Most high-school classes in American history never get to the end of the textbook.

One excuse for giving short, bland accounts of the recent

The Changing Times of Christopher Columbus

Changing times can change our view of the distant past, or *zamani*, as well as the recent past, the *sasha*. Look at the example of Christopher Columbus, whose deeds and legacy are explored in chapter 2.

While Columbus was still in the sasha, Bartolomé de Las Casas and other writers and priests noted the Spaniards' mistreatment and enslavement of Caribbean Indians. Much later, however, Columbus was celebrated as a daring man of science who proved the world was round and opened the Americas to progress. This was the image of Columbus that the United States honored in 1892, on the 400-year anniversary of his landing in the Caribbean. It appealed to a country that was wrapping up 300 years of triumphant warfare against Native Americans.

Things had changed again by 1992, the 500-year anniversary of Columbus's first landing. This time, many celebrations of Columbus were met with protests or countercelebrations, often organized by Native Americans. New histories examined Columbus the exploiter, not just Columbus the explorer. The contrast between the 1892 and 1992 celebrations shows that our understanding of history can change even after hundreds of years. Our view of Columbus changed because *we* had changed.

The "new" Columbus of 1992 was closer to the Columbus of the sasha than to the Columbus of 1892. He was the Columbus of an America that now had to get along with dozens of new nations, many of them governed by people of color, that were once colonies of Spain and other European powers. By 2007, as we have seen, even our textbooks had begun telling of the disasters as well as the benefits that grew out of Columbus's voyages.

past is that it is, well, *recent*. It's too soon to know what historians will say about the period after more time has passed. The passage of time will supposedly provide historical perspective—a more distant, balanced, coolheaded view.

For topics in the zamani, textbook writers use historical perspective as a shield. They write about events in a boring, all-knowing tone. This suggests that there is a single historical truth, upon which historians have agreed. Textbooks will teach it, and students will memorize it. This way of writing also suggests that our historical perspective gets more accurate as more time passes. But the passage of time does not automatically bring a clearer view of events. Information is lost as well as gained over time.

Questions About 9/11

When textbook authors write about the recent past, they do not have to be limited by the lack of historical perspective. In fact, they have advantages.

They lived through the events. They were exposed to news about them. Multiple points of view are available, each backed up by evidence that is more, or less, convincing. Authors can do their own research. They can consult news reports, interview people who made recent history, and share their interpretations with scholars who are studying the events. All of this should help textbook writers cover the recent past in a way that is both interesting and informative.

The terrorist attacks on New York City on 9/11/2001 were in the very recent past for the textbooks I reviewed in the mid-2000s. What did the textbooks say about this event? What *should* they say?

Surely students—like other Americans—want answers to four questions. First, What happened? Second, Why were we attacked? Third, How did we allow it to happen? Those questions lead logically to the fourth question, Will it happen again?

Young readers of this book will not remember 9/11. For you it is in the sasha, the recent past that was experienced by people still living. But textbooks do tell what happened on that day— maybe because that first question is the easiest of the four to answer.

On September 11, 2001, nineteen men hijacked four jets after they had departed from airports in Massachusetts, Virginia, and New Jersey. The hijackers flew two of the planes into the World Trade Center towers in New York City, at that time the second and third tallest buildings in the United States. They

New York's World Trade towers burn after the terrorist attack of 9/11/2001. The attack shocked Americans and launched an unending "war on terror."

flew a third into Washington, DC's Pentagon, the headquarters of the U.S. Department of Defense. The fourth plane crashed in a Pennsylvania field. Passengers on that plane learned from their cell phones of the earlier attacks and tried to overpower the hijackers.

Almost 3,000 people were killed, including all of the hijackers and more than 300 firefighters, police officers, and other first responders in New York. Both of the World Trade Center towers collapsed. Some surrounding buildings were also destroyed or damaged. The Pentagon suffered damage. All air traffic across the country was shut down for several days. The years to come would see sickness and death among people, including rescue workers, who were affected by the widespread smoke and chemical pollution resulting from the attacks.

Osama bin Laden, the Saudi Arabian leader of a terrorist organization known as al-Qaeda, claimed that he was responsible for the attack. The first U.S. response was to attack the Taliban government in Afghanistan.

The Taliban was a fundamentalist Muslim group that our government, through the Central Intelligence Agency, had previously supported. That's because the Taliban had fought against a communist government in Afghanistan that was supported by the Soviet Union. Unfortunately, after coming to power in the country, the Taliban sheltered bin Laden and other terrorists. Although the United States bombed Afghanistan and helped enemies of the Taliban take over the government after the 2001 terrorist attacks, U.S. forces would not get hold of bin Laden until May 2011, when he was shot by U.S. forces who raided his residence in Pakistan.

Where Is the "Why"?

Two of the textbooks I surveyed gave five full pages to the "what happened" question about the 9/11 attacks. How did they handle the "why" question?

The teacher's edition of one said, "Tell students that in this section they will learn about the attacks of September 11, 2001, the economic and social consequences, and the response by Americans and the U.S. government." Not a word about possible causes of the attacks. Only one textbook explained Osama bin Laden's resentment of the United States, giving students information that could help answer the "why" question. The other textbooks left students defenseless against the too-simple explanation offered by our government. Nine days after the attacks, President George W. Bush gave Congress his answer to the "why" question:

> *Americans are asking, why do they hate us? They hate what we see right here in this chamber—a democratically elected government. Their leaders are self-appointed. They hate our freedoms—our freedom of religion, our freedom of speech, our freedom to vote and assemble and disagree with each other.*

What a happy thought—they hate us because we're good! Bush repeated the same message for a year. It caught on, perhaps because it made people feel better.

The notion that terrorists attacked us because of our values or freedoms may soothe our anguish and anger, but it is shallow and inaccurate. Journalist James Fallows pointed this out.

Not Always the Good Guy

Textbooks find it hard to question America's actions in the world because most of them adopt the "international good guy" view of the United States described in chapter 8. One book told students this about "history as a theme":

Fighting for Freedom and Democracy. Throughout the nation's history, Americans have risked their lives to protect their freedoms and to fight for democracy both here and abroad.

The heading "Fighting for Freedom and Democracy" sends a signal that the military history in this book can be viewed only one way. The authors of a different textbook spelled it out. Right after describing the end of our war against Vietnam, they said, "Still a superpower, the United States could not avoid some responsibility for keeping peace in the world. Since the American Revolution, the nation had served as a beacon of hope for people who wanted to govern themselves." The students using this book weren't supposed to notice that the United States had just spent a decade making war to keep Vietnam from governing itself. Such uncritical language makes it hard to understand why al-Qaeda or anyone else would attack a peacekeeping "beacon of hope."

I invite you to do a little research. Here are a few U.S. wars and military interventions in other countries: the Mexican War (1846–48), the Philippine-American War (1899–1902), World War II (1939–45), military intervention in Kosovo (1998–99), the Libyan Civil War (2011), and the Iraq War (2003–11). Which ones would you place under the heading "Fighting for Freedom and Democracy"?

He said, "The soldiers, spies, academics, and diplomats I have interviewed are unanimous in saying 'They hate us for who we are' is dangerous claptrap."

Michael Scheuer agreed. Scheuer was the first chief of the bin Laden unit in the Central Intelligence Agency (CIA). In his words:

> *Bin Laden has been precise in telling America the reasons he is waging war on us. None of the reasons have anything to do with our freedom, liberty, and democracy, but have everything to do with U.S. policies and actions in the Muslim world.*

A Pentagon report in 2004 said the same thing: "Muslims do not 'hate our freedom,' but rather they hate our policies." If we took this seriously, we might question or change our policies in the Middle East. But "they hate us for our freedom" does away with such thoughts.

Where Is the "How"?

Most textbooks also ignored the third question I asked earlier in this chapter: how did we allow the 9/11 attacks to happen? Authors do not want to criticize the U.S. government, but there is plenty of blame to go around. Both Democratic and Republican administrations made mistakes in the years and months before the attacks.

From 1993 to 2001 the administration of President Bill Clinton, a Democrat, took few steps to improve our nation's security against terrorist attacks. In particular, the Immigration and Naturalization Service (INS) was known to be bungling the job of overseeing people from other countries coming into the United States. The INS was unable to create useful lists of people who should not be let in. When visitors overstayed their visas—the permits that told how long they could spend in the United States—the INS did poorly at tracking them. It was not even willing to look for people who had missed court hearings in immigration cases.

George W. Bush, a Republican, became president in January 2001. His administration did even less to make us secure. The textbooks I reviewed, however, did not report on the warnings Bush received before 9/11 but failed to act on. In 2000, the year before the attack, the Clinton administration had staged rescue drills based on the idea of a plane crashing into the Pentagon. This shows that they were aware of the possibility. Yet the Federal Bureau of Investigation (FBI) failed to follow up on reports from some of its agents that suspicious Arabs were training to fly commercial jets in American flying schools. More than a month before the attacks, President Bush received a report titled "Bin Laden Determined to Strike in U.S." He took no action.

Families of people killed in the attacks pressed Congress to look into why the warnings were ignored and why the attacks had not been prevented. Congress created an investigating group called the 9/11 Commission. One textbook I reviewed gave Bush credit for launching the commission. In reality, he was against it. Public opinion forced him to agree to it, but he and his administration cooperated reluctantly. No other textbook even mentioned the commission.

These uncomfortable facts are mostly overlooked when the history of 9/11 is taught. Citizens deserve to be able to understand and discuss what their government has done wrong, and what it can do better. Without information, how will young people become those citizens?

Will It Happen Again?

No one can predict the future. Textbooks cannot answer our fourth question about the 9/11 attacks, Will it happen again? But their tone is upbeat and encouraging.

One book said, "The President moved quickly to combat terrorism at home. Less than a month after 9/11, Bush created the Department of Homeland Security." This is followed by three paragraphs about how the government was reorganized when Homeland Security was created. That textbook was being printed when one of the tragic results of the reorganization came to light during the onslaught of Hurricane Katrina in 2005. It is impossible to say whether the authors would have included Hurricane Katrina if they could.

Hurricane Katrina struck the city of New Orleans, Louisiana, in August 2005. It brought widespread storm damage and serious, long-lasting floods. The government's response to the disaster was late and inadequate. The Federal Emergency Management Agency (FEMA), whose job is to respond to natural disasters with aid, had been part of the reorganization that gave birth to Homeland Security. In that process, FEMA had been made smaller and had lost some of its authority. Hurricane Katrina showed that this drastically limited our national ability to cope with disasters.

The authors of those upbeat paragraphs about the Department of Homeland Security couldn't know that Hurricane Katrina would reveal FEMA's shortcomings. But plenty of other information was available to textbook authors. Experts had widely questioned whether our nation was prepared to deal with terrorist weapons and explosives that might come through its ports. And because fifteen of the nineteen hijackers were from Saudi Arabia, there were also questions about a program that made it especially easy for people from Saudi Arabia to get visas to enter the United States.

These and other problems that Homeland Security had not solved were in the news. They could have been discussed in the most recent textbooks I surveyed. Instead, students were given cheerful words. Upbeat, positive language without uncertainty or questions can be reassuring, but only until the next attack. Then students will feel cheated.

Never Dead

Even more than earlier chapters, the last pages of U.S. history textbooks often come across as just lists of events, one after the other. They rarely offer interpretation of the events, or possible causes and effects. These last pages seem especially lacking in a point of view.

I suspect this is because no one writes them—at least, no one who is hired to have a point of view. History textbooks may feature the names of famous historians or writers on their covers, but you'll see in chapter 12 how these books are often written or updated by underlings. Many of these clerks and free-lance writers have no background in history. They have no time to review what historians, political scientists, and journalists have written. They are hired simply to write summaries of what happened. The pages they produce for textbooks' final chapters have even less style than the rest of these heavy books, and are even less interesting.

We have seen how our history courses and textbooks generally favor the zamani, the distant past, over the sasha, the recent past. This tendency is unfortunate. Students need information about the recent past if they are to fully understand events that are still unfolding around them. Yet most students have no personal memory of history going back more than a few years. Some of today's students are too young to remember when Barack Obama was elected president in 2008. Soon the surprising results of the 2016 election, which made Donald J. Trump president, will be ancient history to the middle schoolers and even high schoolers of tomorrow.

"The past is never dead," wrote American author William Faulkner. "It's not even past." This is absolutely true about the sasha. It may be our most important past, because it is not dead but living-dead. The fact that textbooks and teachers spend so little time on it is the most wicked crime that schools commit against students. It robs them of information and perspective about precisely the issues that most affect their lives.

Half-remembered tidbits about the Battle of Put-in-Bay in the War of 1812 do little to help young people understand the world they enter after leaving school. That world is still working out issues such as gender roles and equal pay. That world faces nations such as India, Pakistan, Iran, and North Korea with growing ability to make nuclear bombs. That world is marked by rising social and economic inequality, both within nations and between nations. Leaving out the recent past means that young people will take away little from their history classes that they can use in that world.

Chapter 11

HISTORY
AND
THE FUTURE

*Americans see history as a straight line
and themselves standing on the cutting edge of it
as representatives for all mankind.*

—FRANCES FITZGERALD

YOU AND I ARE ABOUT TO DO SOMETHING THAT NO American history class has ever accomplished. We will reach the end of the textbook! What final words do our history courses have for their students?

Some of the textbooks I surveyed struck a special note in their last words. *The American Tradition* ended with "the American tradition remains strong—strong enough to meet the many challenges that lie ahead." *The American Adventure* ended with "the American adventure will surely continue." A third textbook ended with these words:

Most Americans remained optimistic about the nation's future. They were convinced that their free institutions, their great natural wealth, and the genius of the American people would enable the U.S. to continue to be—as it always has been—THE LAND OF PROMISE.

ACROSS THE CONTINENT.

Westward the Course of Empire Takes Its Way *has been reproduced in many U.S. history textbooks. The "primitive" Native hunters and fishers on one side of the railroad are contrasted with the bustling white settlers on the other. The picture suggests that progress doomed the Native Americans, so we do not need to look too closely at how the United States took their land.*

That textbook's title was *Land of Promise.*

Even textbooks that don't end with their own titles tend to close with the same empty good cheer. This is another missed opportunity. If textbooks gave students a deep understanding of how events and trends have shaped the past and present, they could end by encouraging students to use what they've learned and project it into the future. What a thrilling way to end a history textbook!

Instead, the students who made it to the end of the textbooks in my survey—if any of them did—found terms like "challenges of the future," "opportunities," and "hope and determination." One response might be, Well, why not give a happy ending? We don't want to depress young people. We can't know what's going to happen next, anyway, so let's end on an upbeat note.

We certainly cannot know what's going to happen next. But the lack of curiosity and intellectual excitement in our history textbooks is *most* noticeable at their ends. "All is well," the authors seem to say in soothing voices. "No need to think about whether the nation and humankind are on the right path. No need to think at all."

Not only is this boring, it is bad history. But the fact that nearly all textbooks end in the same happy, content-free way tells us something. It signals that a social archetype—one of those ideas or beliefs that a society shares, often without putting them into words—is lurking nearby. The social archetype at the end of our history textbooks is progress. It sprouts in the books' first chapters and bursts into full bloom on their final pages.

Progess Is Our Most Important Product

For centuries, progress has been America's big idea. Americans have viewed their history as a demonstration of it.

Thomas Jefferson wrote of an imaginary journey from "the savages of the Rocky Mountains" to the frontiers where people herded livestock, then on to mankind's "most improved state in our seaport towns." Such a journey, he said, was like "the progress of man from the infancy of creation to the present day. And where this progress will stop no one can say."

The idea of progress loomed over American culture in the nineteenth century. It was still being celebrated in 1933, even

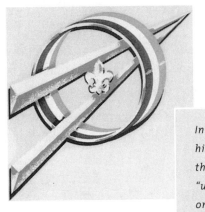

In the 1950s, a design company hired by the Boy Scouts redesigned the Explorer symbol to be more "up to date." The new symbol's onward and upward thrust perfectly captures the archetype of progress.

though the United States was in the midst of the Great Depression, a time of severe economic hardship for many people. A large "world's fair" in Chicago that year was called the Century of Progress Exposition.

In the 1950s, most people took it for granted that *more* meant "better." We boasted about such national accomplishments as the United States having "72% of the world's automobiles, 61% of the world's telephones, and 92% of the world's bathtubs"—all with just 6% of the world's population!

Growth meant progress, and progress provided meaning, in some basic, unthinking way. The future looked brighter yet. Most Americans believed their children would inherit a better planet and enjoy fuller lives.

The authors of the textbooks I reviewed grew up in this America. Even in the newest books, they were still trying to sell it to students. Perhaps textbooks don't question the belief in progress because it fits the way Americans like to think about education—that it leads step by step to opportunity for individuals, which means progress for the nation. The social archetype of progress also provides hope for the future.

History textbooks go even further. They suggest that simply by being part of society, Americans contribute to a nation that is constantly making progress and is the hope of the world. Near the end of one textbook, the authors said, "Americans—makers of something out of nothing—have delivered a new way of life to

Have-Nots or "Developing Nations"?

The language of progress affects the way we talk—and think—about other countries. Instead of rich and poor countries, or haves and have-nots, the world is divided into "developed" and "developing" nations. This vocabulary lets the "developed" nations avoid facing the injustice of the division. After all, aren't the "developing" nations getting better, following in our footsteps?

In reality, development in some countries has been making the developing nations of Asia, Africa, and Latin America poorer, compared with the United States and Europe. In 1850, average national income per person in the United States and Europe was five times greater than in the developing nations of Asia, Africa, and Latin America. By 1960, it was ten times greater. By the early 2000s, the difference ranged from 20 to 60 times.

Yet the vocabulary of progress remains hopeful. A few "developing nations" really are developing—that is, moving closer to the economic and social model of the United States. Others are poverty-stricken and sometimes desperate.

In the nineteenth century, the vocabulary of progress provided an equally splendid explanation for empire building, as the more "advanced" countries seized control of other parts of the world. Europeans and Americans saw themselves as performing useful services, such as running governments and using natural resources, for the natives of distant lands who were too backward to do it for themselves.

the far corners of the world." The social archetype of American exceptionalism, the belief that America is the best country in the world, starts in our textbooks with the Pilgrims, as you saw in chapter 3. At the end of the books, it gets projected into the future.

Faith in progress has certain functions in society, and in our textbooks. It supports and promotes the way things are. We must be doing things right, it says. Look how much progress we've made. This belief has been especially useful to the upper class. Americans could be led to overlook the injustice of social class if they believed the economic pie was getting bigger for everyone.

The social archetype of progress works against change. Things are getting better all the time, so everyone should believe in the system. But is our belief in progress itself changing?

Progress Is Losing Its Grip

Progress has gradually been losing its grip. In 1982, thinkers from various fields of study shared their thoughts on "Progress and Its Discontents." The editors who collected the work into a book said, "Future historians will probably record that from the mid-twentieth century on, it was difficult for anyone to retain faith in the idea of continuing and inevitable progress."

As far as the general public is concerned, opinion polls show that in the early 21st century, not everyone believes that the future will automatically be better than the present. In 2011, only 44% of Americans thought that the next generation would enjoy a higher standard of living. By 2014, that percentage had fallen to 30.

People's general happiness is going down, too. Americans felt themselves to be less happy in 1998 than in 1970, when they had felt less happy than in 1957. By 2014, fewer people said they were "very happy" than in 1998. More said they were "not too happy."

This change did not take place all at once. Intellectuals had been questioning the idea of progress for a long time. During World War I (1914–18), a German historian named Oswald Spengler published *The Decline of the West*. It suggested that Western civilization was beginning an unavoidable downturn. The war itself shook belief in Western progress. So did mass killings in Russia under Joseph Stalin, who was dictator of the Soviet Union from 1929 to 1953. World War II (1939–45) included the Holocaust, the genocidal murder of millions of Jews and others by the Nazi leaders of Germany. These terrible events made many people question the idea of human progress.

By the 1970s, another problem with progress was becoming clear. The number of people in the world was rising. More and more nations were moving toward Western-style industrial economies. These trends caused increases in human use of natural resources such as timber, oil, coal, natural gas, and minerals. In just the twenty years between 1950 and 1970, the world doubled its use of fuel, and its use of electricity increased by seven times.

Progress was bringing other problems as well. One was a growing amount of waste, especially plastic, clogging dumps, landfills, and oceans around the world. Another was that chemical waste from energy producing, mining, manufacturing, and farming was polluting air and water. A third problem was the destruction of natural environments such as wetlands and forests as undeveloped land became roadways, building sites, farms, and logging operations.

Awareness of these problems has increased since the 1970s. Hundreds of organizations now exist with the mission of protecting the environment, wild places, or wildlife. Each April, schools plan special events for Earth Day, a day devoted to environmental awareness. Laws passed in the 1970s have improved air and water quality in the United States and some other countries. Yet the planet we all share is in trouble because of our addiction to growth and to our idea of progress.

The Commons Crisis

One way to think about the downside of progress is to see the world and its resources as a commons. A commons is a piece of land, or some other resource such as a river, that belongs to an entire community and can be used by all.

Imagine a colonial New England town where nearly every family has a cow to provide it with milk and butter. Each morning the cows are taken to the common town pasture. They munch grass all day.

Then a well-off family buys a second cow. That family now has more milk and butter than it needs, so it sells some to people who don't have cows of their own, such as sailors and merchants. *This dairy business is great*, the family thinks. It uses the butter-and-milk money to buy a third cow. A couple of other families buy second cows.

Now more cows than ever are using the pasture. Yet families with two or three cows pay the same amount—nothing—to use the pasture as families with one cow. In time, the once-green pasture is an overgrazed, trampled field of mud. It was useful when twenty cows grazed on it, but 40 or 50 cows ate the grass faster than it could regrow.

This is what social scientists call the tragedy of the commons. The shared resource is public, but the profits are private—they go to individuals (or families, or corporations). Because each individual wants to get the most benefit from the commons, and the biggest users pay no more than the smallest, individuals have no reason to limit their use of the resource.

Today's world has many examples of the commons crisis. One involves fish and shellfish. In 1892, fishers took 20,000,000 bushels of crabs and oysters from the Chesapeake Bay on our East Coast. In 1982, they took 3.5 million bushels. Ten years later, in 1992, the catch had fallen to just 166,000 bushels. The fishers did what people do when their standard of living is threatened: work harder to take more of the few crabs and oysters still out there. This may benefit individual families, but it can only hurt the commons.

The problem of the Chesapeake Bay is playing out in the world's oceans. Demand for seafood is growing along with the planet's population. Technological advances in large-scale fishing keep making it easier for fleets to sweep up enormous numbers of living things from the sea—including bycatch, a term for fish and other animals that are simply thrown away because they are not the desired target.

In 2006 *Science* magazine reported that by 2048, nine-tenths of the species of fish and shellfish that now feed people may be gone. More than a quarter of those species have already collapsed, meaning that their harvests were already less than one-tenth what they had been. Because international waters are involved, treaties and other plans to regulate fishing may not succeed until many other species are extinct.

The economy has become global, and the commons now includes the entire planet. But the economic development we have seen in the United States does not fit with our archetype of progress, which says that what is good for America is good for all humankind. In political terms, we can hope other nations will adopt our forms of democracy and respect for civil liberties. In economic terms, we can only hope that all nations will *not* reach our style of life, because if they did, the earth would become a desert.

We have no way to measure the full effect of humans on the earth. Our increasing power makes it ever more possible that we will make the planet uninhabitable by accident. We almost have, on several occasions. By the mid-1980s, for example, scientists had shown that manufactured chemicals called chlorofluorocarbons (CFCs), used in sprays, refrigerators, and other products, were damaging the earth's upper atmosphere. The CFCs were breaking down a layer of ozone, an element that shields the planet from much of sunlight's destructive ultraviolet radiation.

In the early 1990s, nations around the world agreed to stop making CFCs. An article in the *Washington Post* noted in 2006, "Scientists are haunted by the realization that if CFCs had been made with a slightly different type of chemistry, they'd have destroyed much of the ozone layer over the entire planet." We were simply lucky.

Can We Stop Growing?

The economic development that brought us this far may not guide us to a livable planet in the long run. At some point in the future, perhaps before today's middle schoolers pass their fiftieth birthdays, the United States and other industrialized countries may have to change. Our constantly increasing consumption of energy and raw materials may have to slow down. Our definition of *progress* may have to shift from the upward-pointing arrow of "more, bigger, constant growth" toward a level line.

No family in that New England village thought it would be better off stopping with one cow. In the same way, no nation wants to be the first to achieve a no-growth economy. A new international mechanism may be required, one that is hard even to picture today. If the citizens of tomorrow will have to imagine lesser growth, most middle-school and high-school history courses are doing nothing to prepare them. If textbooks' unthinking devotion to the idea of progress makes students blind to the possibility of doing things differently, change will be that much more difficult. For this reason, our environmental crisis is also an educational problem.

People who write about environmental issues, says biologist Edward O. Wilson, fall into two camps. The environmentalist camp includes most scientists and science writers. The other camp, the exceptionalists, has a few scientists (including some political scientists), economists, and spokespeople for various industries.

Exceptionalists have put forth some important answers to the doom preached by environmentalists. When I wrote the first edition of this book in 1994, I pointed out exceptionalists who compared their world to the world of our ancestors. Modern societies have more power to harm the planet, they said, but they also have more power to set the environment right. Our capitalist economic system and our industrial technology are marvelously flexible.

The exceptionalist view is that the tools of modern Western society will save us. After all, environmental damage has been undone from time to time. Some American rivers that were once believed to be hopelessly polluted are now safe for fish and swimmers. Human activity reforested South Korea. We saved the ozone layer. (Or did we? People's willingness to put their own short-term profits first still threatens the ozone. In 2018, factories in China were still making and using CFCs, and emitting them into the atmosphere, even though everyone knew the danger.)

In 1994 I criticized textbooks for not giving students *either* the exceptionalist *or* the environmentalist side of this debate. They should present both points of view, I felt, and teachers could then encourage students to think about them. Not only should textbooks present the very real looming problems, but they should show how various societies have solved problems and adapted to changing conditions.

No longer do I suggest this evenhanded approach. Our current crisis cannot be solved by the very things that have created it. What has changed?

The Climate Future

Our current crisis is new in at least two ways. First, we face a permanent shortage of fossil fuels: oil, natural gas, and coal.

The Arctic is warming faster than other parts of the planet. Threatened by melting polar ice and rising temperatures, polar bears are at risk of extinction—along with many other species suffering from climate change.

These are not renewable. Fracking has increased the supply, but still it is finite. Once used, these fuels are gone for good.

Great advances have been made in harnessing renewable energy sources, such as wind and solar energy, but we are still far from being able to power the households and cities of the world from such sources—let alone its jet airplanes and industrial plants. The fossil-fuel shortage, whenever it arrives, will probably be an energy shortage. Certainly it will affect products such as plastics, chemicals, and fertilizers.

Second, our use of fossil fuels is having a serious worldwide impact: global warming. Ice at the poles and everywhere else on earth is melting, causing sea levels to rise. In the 2000s the

The world's population was 7.6 billion in 2017, according to the United Nations. It is projected to rise through the 21st century. How many people can the earth support?

administration of President George W. Bush accepted the prediction that the world's oceans will rise three feet in the 21st century. Around the world, from Miami Beach to Bangladesh, hundreds of millions of people who live near sea level will lose their homes and livelihoods. This global upheaval will be the biggest crisis humankind has faced since the beginning of recorded history.

And that is the most pleasant estimate. Many climate researchers now fear that global warming poses a bigger threat to the ice of Greenland and Antarctica than they previously thought. The least pleasant estimates say that water levels may rise by several dozen feet, or more. And the effects of the warming will continue

The Lesson of Haiti

History reveals many once-healthy societies whose ecosystems were damaged perhaps beyond repair. One of them is Haiti, in the Caribbean.

On first seeing Haiti, Christopher Columbus praised "the beauty of the land." He and other Spaniards then introduced new diseases, plants, and livestock. Their pigs, hunting dogs, and horses multiplied quickly, causing tremendous environmental damage. A Spanish settler wrote in 1518 that "these islands had been, since God made the earth, prosperous and full of people lacking nothing they needed." But after the Europeans arrived, he added, "they were laid waste, inhabited only by wild animals and birds."

Later, gardening for food gave way to large-scale plantation farming of a single crop, sugarcane, for quick profit. Intensive use of the soil, without rotating crops, made the soil less fertile. More recently, population growth has caused people to cut trees so they can farm the steep hillsides of the island. As a result, rains have eroded the topsoil.

Today an island ecosystem that once supported a large population is in far worse shape than when Columbus first saw it. This sad story may predict the future, now that modern technology has the power to make the whole earth a Haiti.

for centuries, even if the human race stops increasing its use of fossil fuels right now.

To expect textbooks published around 1990 to cover global warming might not be fair. So how did the six newer textbooks in my survey handle the subject? Only two of them mention it at all. One gave it a single sentence, saying that "air pollution could be a factor." Another gave a paragraph to the subject of "developments like global warming." It said nothing about the future. It did, though, reassuringly point out that "Americans took pride in the efforts they had made to clean up their own turf."

THE MASSACRE OF THE TREES.

The 1907 drawing Massacre of the Trees *captures the idea that people are meant to dominate nature and use its resources. The idea is one cornerstone of the American belief in progress. The small figures scattered on the forest floor are "Dummy Homesteaders"—possibly representing people too small and weak to conquer nature.* (Christopher Michel)

Why was the treatment of environmental issues in these textbooks so feeble? Is it because if authors changed their closing pages and ditched the unthinking praise of progress, those pages would no longer fit the tone of heroic celebration that fills the rest of the book? Progress is the plotline of the textbooks' story. Our nation is presented as getting better in all areas, from race relations to transportation to the environment. There may have been some problems and setbacks, a few bumps in the road here and there—but America has overcome them and kept moving forward.

The Siren Song of Progress

Like the Sirens of Greek legends, whose beautiful songs lured sailors to their doom, the song of progress lulls us into thinking that everything now is "advanced." It also tempts us to think that long-ago societies were more "primitive" than they may have been.

This is unfortunate. We may never learn that some of our present-day goals, such as equal treatment of men and women, have been achieved by other peoples. Many things about modern life are far better than what existed before, but that isn't always true. Take the way Americans feed our babies.

At some point we convinced ourselves that packaged "formula" or even cow's milk was a more modern, advanced way to feed infants than the age-old method of breast-feeding. By 1992, only half of all women who gave birth in U.S. hospitals breast-fed their babies. Since then we have rediscovered something that "primitive" societies never forgot—that human babies evolved to flourish on human milk.

In the same way, belief in progress can keep students from seeing value in present-day societies different from our own. If we think our own society is the best and most progressive, it may be natural to think we have nothing to learn from other cultures.

History and social studies courses could help open young people to ideas from other cultures—but that doesn't happen, because the idea of progress is built into these courses from Columbus to their final words.

If textbooks gave up their blind devotion to the archetype of progress, they could invite young people to weigh technol-

Vietnam
veteran's hat

★ HISTORY
AND ART *Problem We All Live With* by
Norman Rockwell Postwar America
faced increasing tension over racial discrimination—a
critical situation that affected all Americans, young
and old alike.

*Textbooks can ruin even powerful images by the way they misuse
them. This spread from* The American Journey *features a famous
Norman Rockwell painting called* The Problem We All Live With.
*It shows an African American girl neatly dressed for the first day
of school, with federal marshals walking in front of and behind
her to protect her from racist violence. Unfortunately, we don't
see the painting well, because the spread is cluttered with a
picture of a hat, an automobile ad, and a picture of a button,
and she is walking into the gutter between pages.*

ogies and practices from other cultures. Instead of assuming
that our ways simply must be the best, they could challenge students to think anew about everything from the American way
of birth to the American way of death. They could even encourage debate about different ways of defining *progress*. Then the
closing chapters of history textbooks would become exercises
in investigation and thought, guiding students toward facts and
resources on all sides of important issues. Surely this would do

more to prepare students for the rest of their lives than mindlessly upbeat endings.

One of the newer textbooks in my survey, *The American Pageant*, did give some serious treatment to our future. Its next-to-last page spoke of such environmental worries as pollution, global warming, and the energy crisis. So far, so good. At least that page raised the issues and did not suggest that they were nothing to worry about.

Unfortunately, on its very last page, *Pageant* said, "In facing those challenges, the world's oldest republic had an extraordinary tradition of resilience and resourcefulness to draw on." Many young people are not so easily reassured. A 1993 survey found that children were much more concerned about the environment than their parents. A survey of high-school seniors in 1999 found that almost half of them believed "the best years of the United States were behind us." By 2014, about half of the general public agreed.

The upbeat, happy endings in our textbooks send a message about history itself. By avoiding serious discussion of trends in our past, by raising no real questions about the future, the authors suggest that our past has no effect on our future. We can hardly blame students for concluding that history—at least as it is taught in school—has nothing to do with their own lives to come.

Chapter 12

DOES THIS WAY OF TEACHING HISTORY WORK?

When you're publishing a book, if there's something that is controversial, it's better to take it out.

—Representative of Holt, Rinehart and Winston, a textbook publisher

IF YOU HAVE READ THE ELEVEN CHAPTERS BEFORE this one, you've seen that the textbooks I reviewed supplied young people with a lot of unnecessary and even wrong details. At the same time, they left out key questions and facts about everything from Columbus's second voyage to the fate of our environment.

You have also seen that the textbooks gave their readers no chance to use what they have learned about the past to understand the issues of the present—much less to think intelligently about the future. Textbooks rarely present the various sides of a historical controversy, such as the debate about early voyages to the Americas that is described in chapter 1. And they almost never reveal to students the evidence for different interpretations.

Yet these textbooks must be satisfying somebody. Who?

Publishers of textbooks have several audiences in mind—not just the young people who will use the books in school, but also teachers, historians, college professors of history, politicians, and the general public. That public includes parents—whom publishers do not want to upset.

Some members of the public have not been shy about what they want textbooks to do. In 1925 the American Legion claimed that the ideal U.S. history textbook would "inspire the children with patriotism," "speak chiefly of success," and make sure to include the achievements of each state.

In contrast, Shirley Engle and Anna Ochoa, experts in social studies education, described the ideal textbook in 1986. They felt that it should "confront students with important questions and problems for which answers are not readily available" and use "data from a variety of sources such as history, the social sciences, literature, journalism, and from students' firsthand experiences."

The textbooks in my survey were much closer to the old American Legion ideal than to the more modern one. The secondary literature in American history—the published work of historians, based on primary sources—was not to blame. Largely because of the civil rights movement and its impact, the secondary literature has become broad, inclusive, and accurate. Yet even the newer textbooks in my survey did not take advantage of the readily available research that I used to write this book. Historian Marc Ferro argued in 1981 that the United States had the largest gap of any country between what historians knew and what the rest of us were taught.

As we have seen throughout this book, our society sometimes lies to itself about our past, or at least turns away from

Protecting Children

We should present a "nice" version of history to protect children from unpleasantness—or so some people think. Why confront young people with issues that even adults cannot settle? To choose just one example, must we tell fifth-graders the gruesome details of what Columbus did on Haiti?

Perhaps a fifth- or even twelfth grader who sees illustrations of Spaniards cutting off American Indians' hands, or of Indians committing suicide, will have nightmares about Columbus. But if we sanitize Columbus, we leave out important parts of the story that would help young people understand the history that flowed from Columbus's actions.

I doubt that shielding children from violence is the real reason textbooks leave out things. Textbooks *do* include violence, after all, as long as it isn't by "us." Look at how *American History* described John Brown's actions at Pottawatomie, Kansas, in 1856:

> In the dead of night, they entered the cabins of three unsuspecting families. For no apparent reason they murdered five people. They split open their skulls with heavy, razor-edged swords. They even cut off the hand of one of their victims.

You saw in chapter 6 how a textbook author's choice of words to describe Brown painted a picture of him that is far from factual. Here is another example. Details such as the splitting of skulls and the weight of swords make us find Brown revolting. Phrases such as "dead of night," "unsuspecting families," and "no apparent reason" also help build a strongly negative portrait of Brown.

The hands of the Arawak people are much more historically significant. When Columbus cut them off, it was part of an overall system of oppression. It helped strip Haiti of its Native population. *American History* said nothing about Columbus's atrocities. It cannot claim to be even-handed!

the full truth. Perhaps our textbooks only reflect those lies and half-truths because we want them to. That may also be why textbooks avoid controversial subjects. In national public opinion polls, at least half of Americans agree that "books that contain dangerous ideas should be banned from public school libraries." Yet who gets to say what is "dangerous"? Very few people tell me that *they* want to be lied to. Usually they think *other* people—especially young people—need to be lied to "for their own good" or "because they can't handle the truth."

In his novel *1984*, English writer George Orwell said, "Who controls the present controls the past." He meant that those in power shape the way history is told, written—and taught. By choosing what to put in and what to leave out, authors of history textbooks do, in a way, control the past. Keep that in mind as you study history. Ask yourself, What kind of picture of the past are textbooks painting? Why?

Who Really Writes Textbooks?

You may be surprised to learn that the names on the covers of history textbooks are rarely the names of the people who actually wrote the books. It's not always clear who the real authors are.

Take *Rise of the American Nation*, by Lewis Todd and Merle Curti, for example. They may indeed have written the original edition of the book, which was published in 1941. But the tenth edition, which I surveyed, came out in 1991 under the title *Triumph of the American Nation*. By that time, Curti was 95 and in a nursing home, and Todd was dead. They had nothing to do with the changes and new material in "their" book, even though their names remained as the book's authors.

Because the Todd-Curti book sold well in the 1970s and 1980s, its publisher, Holt, wanted to keep it in print. After the 1991 edition, Holt could no longer pretend that Todd and Curti were involved, so in 1994 they moved those recognizable names into a new title, *Todd and Curti's American Nation*. The historian who was hired as its "author" would not tell me how much, if any, of the book he had written. The book came out again in 1998, this time with Todd's and Curti's names dropped from the title. By 2003, the book was called simply *Holt American Nation*. This carried a certain honesty, because the publisher, not the "author," surely wrote most of it.

Publishers hire freelance writers to do much of the work. A woman who had ghostwritten elementary-level textbooks in several subjects told me, "It is absolutely the standard practice in the textbook publishing industry to assign ALL the writing to freelancers. Then you rent a name to go on the cover." One textbook editor, speaking about the real authors, told me, "They pick up things pretty quickly, and in a couple of days, they're up on the Civil War."

Authors who *do* write their own books write only the central narrative. This is becoming a smaller and smaller part of the whole book. Authors have nothing to do with the countless boxes, teaching aids, study questions, photo captions, and "activities" that now often take up more space in history textbooks than the narrative itself.

Publishers use nationalism, not historical scholarship, to sell their books. Covers display national symbols such as the American flag or the Statue of Liberty. The books are marketed as tools for helping students "discover" our "common beliefs" and "appreciate our heritage." No publisher has ever tried to sell a textbook with the claim that it was more accurate than its competitors.

History Is Different

History is different from every other subject you study in school. Textbooks in subjects like math or geology are based on the body of knowledge held by professionals in those fields. History textbooks are, too, but only up to a point.

One textbook publisher said, "[T]extbooks mirror our society and contain what that society considers acceptable." Society doesn't influence what goes into a math textbook. Geology doesn't change when social trends do. History is more personal than math, geology, or even American literature. It is about "us." It is our tool for understanding not just the past but where we are today, and why.

Maybe the fact that history is about us is a reason *not* to teach it honestly to children. Who doesn't want children to be optimists, people who see and expect only the best? Presenting history as an uplifting parade of progress supposedly inspires young people with idealism. Textbooks that focus on our wonderful and fair society may fill them with the desire to live up to it. And then, when students grow up and learn about some of the darker sides of our history, they may want to change the system to make it more like the ideal they were taught.

The problem is that most people never study American history after they leave school. When are they supposed to learn the full picture of our past? Another problem with this plan is that it often backfires. People don't always like finding out that textbooks and teachers have been lying to them.

One of my students wrote about how she had been taught the old story about George Washington using a hatchet to chop down his father's cherry tree, then bravely telling the truth

In 1939 American artist Grant Wood painted Parson Weems,
the author of a book about George Washington, revealing
the fable of the chopped-down cherry tree—which Weems
invented or plagiarized.

about it. Unfortunately, that legend was made up a few years
after Washington's death by Mason Weems, who wrote a book
about the first president. My student later discovered, to her
horror, that "a story I had held sacred in my memory for so long
had been a lie." She felt "bitter and betrayed" by the teachers
who had passed on a false, old story to build up Washington's
image. It made her "question all I had learned."

Bitterness over the cherry tree lie is bad enough. Imagine
how African American kids feel when they learn another truth
about the Founding Fathers. "When I first learned that Washington and Jefferson had slaves, I was devastated," historian
Mark Lloyd told me. "I didn't want to have anything more to do
with them."

Lying to young people is a slippery slope. Once we have started sliding down it, how and when do we stop? Who decides when to lie, and which lies to tell to which age-group? How do we decide what to teach in American history once authors—and publishers, and teachers, and the public—have decided not to value the truth? And why should children believe what they learn in American history if their textbooks are full of lies? Why should they bother to learn it?

Luckily, they don't.

Unlearned History

All over America, students sit in American history and social studies classes. They look at their textbooks and write answers to the 50 questions at the end of each chapter. Then they take quizzes and exams that test how well they have memorized facts.

Here's an example of those facts from one of the textbooks in my survey, *The American Journey*. A "Time Line Activity" asked students to arrange these events in the order in which they happened:

* Serbs, Croats, and Bosnian Muslims sign peace agreement to end civil war
* Soviet Union dissolves
* Bill Clinton is elected to first term as president
* Geraldine Ferraro is first woman from a major political party to run for vice president
* Iraq invades Kuwait
* Sandra Day O'Connor is named to Supreme Court
* Ronald Reagan is reelected president

I lived through all of these events, but I cannot put them in the correct order without looking them up. I am sure the authors of the textbook couldn't, either. Why should anyone memorize whether Reagan appointed O'Connor in his first term or his second?

What matters about these events is their significance in the sweep of history, how they were caused by earlier events and in turn caused later events. Who wants to learn a lot of useless details like dates?

Not students! Study after study shows that they successfully resist learning "facts" like these. When two-thirds of seventeen-year-old Americans cannot place the Civil War in the right half-century, or 22% of my students say that North and South Korea fought the Vietnam War, we are dealing with something more than simply ignorance. This is resistance raised to a high level.

Our usual way of teaching history is not working. Young people are simply not learning even those details of U.S. history that educated Americans *should* know. They learn even less about what *caused* the major developments in our past. This makes it impossible for them to apply lessons from our past to current issues.

How could we teach history differently?

For one thing, we could include emotion. It is the glue that causes history to stick. Our history is a heartrending, passion-filled subject. Students are moved when they read "the good stuff" in voices from our past—the voices of people such as Bartolomé de Las Casas, or Helen Keller, or the soldiers who freed prisoners from the Nazi death camps of World War II. More voices like that could reveal the drama of history while being fair and accurate.

Another way to make history stick is to show how it touches

History texts could include more voices of heroes such as Bartolomé de Las Casas, who strove to protect Native Americans from the Spanish conquerors.

students' own lives. Some inventive teachers have found ways to do this. For example, to show how racism affects African Americans, a teacher in Iowa divided her all-white class of third graders into groups by eye color. For a day, she favored the blue-eyed children and discriminated against the brown-eyed ones, then on the next day she switched to favoring the brown-eyed. The movie *A Class Divided* shows how vividly those students remembered the lesson fifteen years later. Material from American history textbooks is rarely remembered fifteen *days* after the end of the school year.

Students have short-term reasons for accepting what their teachers and textbooks tell them about American history. They are going to be tested on it. Some of them feel a sense of accomplishment in learning something, even something as useless as a series of dates from a "Time Line Activity." Arguing for other points of view or different interpretations takes energy. It probably won't help a student's grade. It might even break class rules or customs. So students themselves may resist changes in the way history is taught, especially if they require more work or more independent thinking. After years of simply memorizing and coughing up facts, students can get used to it. They haven't learned other ways to learn.

In the long run, though, "learning" history this way is not really satisfying. Most history textbooks, and too many high-

In 2018, U.S. Immigration and Customs Enforcement (ICE) stepped up its raids on people suspected of being undocumented immigrants. It also began imprisoning the children of asylum seekers at the U.S. border. People across the land—including many young people—took to the streets in protest.

school history teachers, give young people no reason to love the subject. That's why students rank history as their least-favorite subject time after time. But the sorry state of learning in most history classrooms could change. *You* can make a difference! Remember that student I told you about at the beginning of the book, who used *Lies My Teacher Told Me* to "heckle [his] history teacher from the back of the room"? You can use this version the same way.

History is tremendously interesting. It is also vitally important—especially to young people, because they have a lot of future ahead of them. They deserve an education that relates our past to them and their futures. Students will start finding history interesting when their teachers stop lying to them. They will start learning history when they see the point of doing so.

THE FUTURE
LIES AHEAD—
AND WHAT
TO DO
ABOUT THEM

Once you have learned how to ask questions . . .
you have learned how to learn and no one can keep you
from learning whatever you want or need to know.

—Neil Postman and
Charles Weingartner

What about the next lie? Bad information will soon be passed on to you, and not just by textbooks. It may turn up in a historical marker by the side of a road or a museum exhibit. It may be part of a movie, TV series, or novel about the American past. What can you do about these future lies?

The answer is for all of us to become independent learners. Everyone should know how to sift through arguments and evidence, and how to think through our decisions based upon them. Then we will have learned how to learn, and no one-sided book or argument will be able to confuse us.

For this to happen, schools must help us learn how to ask questions about our society and its history. They must show us how to figure out answers for ourselves. Most American history textbooks and classes fail miserably at this important task.

Sometimes the information in textbooks is completely true. Sometimes it is flatly wrong. And sometimes we—the community of scholars—just don't know for sure. Chapter 2 raised the question of whether sailors from Africa reached the Americas before Europeans did. This is one of many cases where we don't know for sure. Textbooks and teachers should not present such items as facts or leave them out as falsehoods. Instead, they should present them as what they are: historical questions and uncertainties. Students could learn how to pull together evidence on each side, come to a conclusion, but still have room for doubt.

Thousands of topics now clutter our textbooks. There seems to be no room for introducing issues and controversies, teaching young people how to find and use evidence such as primary sources, and letting them practice the skills of logical thinking. We must teach fewer topics but explore them more thoroughly.

What would that look like? To take one example, students have traditionally had to memorize a list of explorers such as Amerigo Vespucci and Ponce de León, with a few words about each one, such as "gave his name to the Americas," or "searched for the Fountain of Youth." What if, instead, students were encouraged to look at the larger picture—how Columbus's 1493 expedition affected Haiti and Spain, as discussed in chapter 3? From there they could examine the effects of Columbus's voyages on the Americas and the world.

Perhaps not everyone in a classroom will come to the same conclusion. Teachers need to be comfortable with the possibility of disagreement, as long as students back up their conclusions with serious historical work. They must make logical arguments based on good evidence.

Question Everything

Whether you are dealing with a textbook, looking up facts online, or visiting a museum, you need to know how to weigh the sources of your information. Here are five questions you can ask about any source of information on American history.

1. When and why was it written or created? Think about who the audience was, where the audience fit into the social structure, and what the writer or speaker was trying to accomplish with them.

2. Whose point of view is presented? Find out where the writer or speaker fit into the social structure. Think about whether the source promotes a particular viewpoint or set of ideas. Ask yourself whose points of view were left out.

3. Is the source believable? Is it internally consistent? Or do statements within it contradict each other? Are people shown acting in a reasonable way? If not, why not?

4. Is the source backed up by other reliable sources? An unsupported claim on someone's website is less reliable than a statistic or quote from an established source—such as a report from a government agency, a book put out by a major publisher, or a newspaper—that you can check. If you are reading a book by a historian, check the author's background. Find out if other historians agree.

5. Finally, how you do think the words or pictures presented by your source want you to feel about America? Words and images have emotional power. Do you think the author or creator was trying to influence your emotions?

If you keep these five questions in mind, you will have learned how to learn history.

"Icy Stares"? Or Helping Hands?

UNION ARMY PASSES ROCKY SPRINGS

Upon the occupation of Willow Springs on May 3, 1863, Union Gen. J. A. McClernand sent patrols up the Jackson road. These groups rode through Rocky Springs, where they encountered no resistance beyond the icy stares of the people who gathered at the side of the road to watch.

On May 5, Gen. P. J. Osterhaus' division stopped briefly at Rocky Springs, while en route to Big Sand Creek. The next day, Gen. A. P. Hovey's division arrived and spent the night. From May 7, when Gen. U. S. Grant began his drive toward the Southern Railroad of Mississippi until May 16 when Gen. H. Ewing's brigade passed through hurrying to overtake the army, the Yankees were never far away. During this period 45,000 blueclad invaders and uncounted wagons had passed along this road.

Throughout the United States, roadside markers, monuments, and museums often give misleading views of history. This marker used to stand along a roadway in southwest Mississippi. Like many markers and monuments across the South, it presented a picture of Southerners as united in supporting the Confederacy and bitterly opposed to the Union. That was false.

In reality, Union general Grant was able to abandon his supply lines and attack Vicksburg because of support from black people in southwestern Mississippi—and some white people, too. Despite the words of this marker, "the people" Grant's forces met helped "the blueclad invaders" by giving them food, showing them the best roads, and telling them where the Confederates were.

I criticized this marker in the first edition of *Lies*. By the year 2000 it had been removed. Maybe your class could examine markers and monuments in your own community. Decide which is the least accurate, then write a more accurate memorial to stand next to it. Your class might even decide to raise money to put it up. In the process, you'll discover some of the ways our historical memory is shaped and made into part of the landscape.

Here teachers and textbooks could do something important and necessary. They could help students understand the difference between opinion and fact. People have a right to their own opinions, but not to their own facts. Opinions not supported by evidence can't be given much weight. Evidence must be based on facts that other people can check for themselves—and then go on to check the sources of *those* facts, if there is doubt.

Young people can bring about change, even if teachers and textbooks don't change much. Students in a Kansas school got their own principal fired after researching her background. Students in the suburbs of Denver left their high schools and protested their own school board, which had attacked the Advanced Placement U.S. History curriculum. The school board had claimed the curriculum was not nationalistic enough. Eventually voters removed the board members. Two Native American students got the state of Minnesota to drop the word *squaw*, an insulting term for a Native woman, from its geographic names.

In the years since I wrote the first edition of *Lies*, the internet has become a powerful tool. For many people, it is the main source of information—or misinformation—about their nation and the world. But whether people get their news and ideas from the internet, television news, or newspapers, it is easier than ever to take in only news and ideas that go along with our own views of the world.

We live in a time when some people question the very idea of *truth*. At times it is hard to find solid ground of facts on which to stand. When people say to me that there's no such thing as truth, I sometimes say, "Right! And the Civil War began in 1876, in Nevada. It grew from a pay dispute between the Union Pacific Railroad and its Chinese workers."

Does this headline make you think that Hillary Clinton lost the popular vote in the 2016 election, and that 25 million fraudulent votes were cast? If you think so, you've been fooled. The headline about Clinton and the story are completely false. They appeared on a website called YourNews Wire.com, which mixes some real news stories with other stories that are entirely made up. At a time when phrases such as "fake news" and "alternative facts" are part of public life, citizens of all ages should master the skills of checking facts, weighing and comparing news sources, and thinking critically.

"B-but that's not true!" comes the reply.

"Bingo!" I reply. There is a bedrock of fact. The Civil War started in 1861 in South Carolina. It had nothing to do with any railroad or Chinese Americans.

That example is about details that are easy to check. What about a harder question, one where there may be room for different interpretations? Here is a question raised in chapter 5 of this book: why did Southern states secede, leading to the Civil

*The crowds at the inaugurations of two U.S. presidents—
Barack Obama in 2009 (left) and Donald Trump in 2017
(right)—were photographed from the same viewpoint. The
difference is clear, yet the Trump White House insisted that
the 2017 crowd was the largest in history. This claim was
one of many disputes about "alternative facts" and "fake
news" during the Trump administration.*

War? I have asked audiences across the United States to answer
it. People always give four answers: for slavery, for states' rights,
because Lincoln was elected, and over financial issues such
as tariffs and taxes. Then I ask the audience to choose their
best single answer. Until 2015, about 20% of people across the
country voted for slavery, 60 to 70% for states' rights, 2% for
the election of Lincoln, and 10 to 18% for financial matters. If
we did history by majority vote, states' rights would be the clear
winner.

Young Japanese-American women, unable to leave the camp where they and their families were confined during World War II, pass the time with volleyball. A little recreation does not change the fact that tens of thousands of Americans of Japanese descent were unjustly held for months or years in bleak, isolated internment camps like this one at Manzanar, California.

In the world of evidence, however, state' rights is the clear loser. As chapter 5 shows, the Southern states that left the Union made their reason perfectly clear. "Our position is thoroughly identified with the institution of slavery," announced Mississippi, and every other state said the same thing. The evidence comes from many sources. Secession was all about racial enslavement and the idea system of white supremacy that supported it. Textbooks and other sources that give states' rights equal weight with slavery may seem "even-handed," but this kind of even-handedness is bad history.

Students, teachers, parents, and citizens are beginning to demand more truthful textbooks—and change does happen. Achieving justice in the present helps us tell the truth about the past. One example is the way textbooks over time covered a shameful episode during World War II. A few months after Japan's attack on Pearl Harbor, the U.S. government "interned" Japanese Americans who lived on the West Coast, forcing them into guarded camps. Most history textbooks of the 1960s ignored this policy, or mentioned it in a short paragraph. By 2007, they did much better. This improvement surely reflected the change in our national view of the events. In 1988 we had passed a law that called the internments a "grave injustice" and awarded $20,000 to each survivor.

It works the other way, too—telling the truth about the past helps achieve justice in the present. For example, when towns understand that during the nadir of race relations they became sundown towns, they sometimes take steps to become less racist today. Just as the state of Mississippi had used bad history as a weapon against my Tougaloo students, you can use accurate history to support positive social change.

History is central to our understanding of ourselves and our society. All Americans should be able to command the power of history. They should know basic facts about the United States and understand the historical processes that have shaped those facts. They should also know some of the social forces and ideas that have affected their own lives. These Americans are then ready to become citizens.

Thomas Jefferson urged the teaching of political history so that Americans could learn "how to judge for themselves what will secure or endanger their freedom." Citizens who are their own historians, who can identify lies and half-truths and who can use sources to find out what really went on in the past, are a powerful force for democracy. After all my years of research and writing, my own journey to know our American past has only begun. After reading all this way, so has yours. Good travels to us both!

Notes

Introduction: Why I Wrote This Book—and Other Questions Answered

ix *"If you truly want students"*: Dudley Lewis, "Teaching the Truth," *San Francisco Examiner & Chronicle*, November 26, 1995.

x *If they can avoid it, they do*: Lewis.

Chapter 1: The Problem with Making Heroes

1 *"What passes for identity in America"*: James Baldwin, "A Talk to Teachers," *Saturday Review*, December 21, 1963, reprinted in Rick Simonson and Scott Walker, eds., *Multi-cultural Literacy* (St. Paul, MN: Graywolf Press, 1998), 9.

3 *"the coming dawn"*: Helen Keller, "Onward, Comrades," address at the Rand School of Social Sciences, New York, December 31, 1920, reprinted in Philip S. Foner, ed., *Helen Keller: Her Socialist Years* (New York: International Publishers, 1967), 107.

4 *"May the sense of serving mankind"*: Foner, 17–18. The United States did not allow Flynn to receive Keller's letter.

7 *No evidence suggests that Wilson was at all reluctant*: Hans Schmidt, *The United States Occupation of Haiti, 1915–1934* (New Brunswick, NJ: Rutgers University Press, 1971), 66, 74.

7 *Historian Walter Karp has shown*: Walter Karp, *The Politics of War* (New York: Harper & Row, 1979), 158–67.

7 *"to be an apostle of the night"*: *Address of President Wilson*, 66th Congress, Senate Document 120 (Washington, DC: Government Printing Office, 1919), 133.

7   *Wilson refused to listen*: Jean Lacouture, *Ho Chi Minh* (New York: Random House, 1968), 24, 265.

10   *America's first epic movie*: Wyn C. Wade, *The Fiery Cross* (New York: Simon & Schuster, 1987), 115–51.

10   *"It is like writing history with lightning"*: Wade, 135–37.

10   *a wave of antiblack riots*: Lerone Bennett Jr., *Before the Mayflower* (Baltimore, MD: Penguin, 1966 [1962]), 292–94. Bennett counts 26 major race riots in 1919 alone. Also see Herbert Shapiro, *White Violence and Black Response* (Amherst, MA: University of Massachusetts Press, 1988), 123–54.

11   *Wilson's attorney general asked him to pardon Debs*: Karp, 326–28; Charles D. Ameringer, *U.S. Foreign Intelligence* (Lexington, MA: D.C. Heath, 1990), 109.

13   *In the early 1920s*: Bessie Pierce, *Public Opinion and the Teaching of History in the United States* (New York: Alfred A. Knopf, 1926), p. 332.

14   *About her socialism . . . "Keller embraced a variety of social causes"*: aoc.gov/sites/default/files/keller_2011.pdf.

14   *"I once believed"*: Helen Keller, *Midstream: My Later Life* (New York: Greenwood, 1968 [1929]), 156.

15   *"People do not like to think"*: Quoted in Jonathan Kozol, *The Night Is Dark and I Am Far From Home* (New York: Simon & Schuster, 1990 [1975]), 101.

16   *"Care should be taken"*: Quoted in Claudia Bushman, "America Discovers Columbus" (Costa Mesa, CA: American Studies Association Annual Meeting, 1992), 9.

Chapter 2: What Did Columbus Really Do?

19   *People from other continents*: David Quinn, *England and the Discovery of America, 1481–1620* (New York:. Knopf, 1974), 5–105; Robert Blow, *Abroad in America* (New York: Continuum, 1990), 17; Jack Forbes, *Black Africans and Native Americans* (Oxford: Basil Blackwell, 1988), 20.

20   *Some archaeologists think that ancient Roman*: Current Anthropol-

ogy 21, no. 1 (February 1980) contains arguments for and against coins as evidence of Roman visits.

20 *Native Americans also crossed*: Forbes, 19; William Fitzhugh, personal communication, November 16, 1993: Ivan Van Sertima, *They Came Before Columbus* (New York: Random House, 1976), chapter 12. See also Alice B. Kehoe, "Small Boats Upon the North Atlantic," in Carroll Riley et al., eds., *Man Across the Sea* (Austin: University of Texas Press, 1971).

20 *history is not a set of facts*: James West Davidson and Mark H. Lytle, *After the Fact* (New York: McGraw-Hill, 1992).

21 *They look like realistic portraits of West Africans*: Van Sertima, 30.

23 *Most textbooks in my survey did mention . . . and maybe of North America*: Forbes, 19; Morgan Llywelyn, "The Norse Discovery of the New World," *Early Man* 2, no. 4 (1980), 3–6; Marshall McKusick and Erik Wahlgren, "Viking in America—Fact and Fiction," *Early Man* 2, no. 4 (1980), 7–9; Charles Duff, *The Truth about Columbus* (London: Jarrold, 1957), 9–13.

24 *First, the West Africans . . . what is now Brazil*: Pathe Diagne, "*Du Centenaire de la Decouverte du Nouveau Monde par Bakari II, en 1312, et Christoper Colomb, en 1491*" (Dakar: privately printed, 1990), 2–3; Van Sertima, 6; Forbes, 13–14.

24 *In the modern era, corpses*: Van Sertima, 21, 26; John L. Sorenson and Martin H. Raish, *Pre-Columbian Contact with the Americas Across the Oceans* (Provo, UT: Research Press, 1990), entry H344; Richard Hoeppli, "Parasitic Diseases in Africa and the Western Hemisphere," in *Acta Tropica*, Supplementum 10 (Basel: Verlag für Recht und Gesellschaft, n.d.), 54–59.

24 *The second set of voyages . . . Iceland's volcanoes*: Riley, *Man Across the Sea*, especially Kehoe, "Small Boats Upon the North Atlantic," 275–92.

25 *Prince Henry knew of these Phoenician voyages*: Constance Irwin, *Fair Gods and Stone Faces* (New York: St. Martin's, 1963), 193–211, 217, 241; Cyrus Gordon, *Before Columbus* (New York: Crown, 1971), 119–25; Geoffrey Ashe et al., *The Quest for America* (London: Pall Mall, 1971), 78–79.

25 *Even the Portuguese word* caravel: Smithsonian Institution, "Seeds

of Change" exhibit (Washington, DC: National Museum of Natural History, 1991).

27   *Advances in military technology*: William H. McNeill, *The Age of Gunpowder Empires* (Washington, DC: American Historical Association, 1989).

28   *"Gold is most excellent"*: Christopher Columbus, letter to the king and queen of Spain, July 1503, in R.H. Major, trans. and ed., *Select Letters of Christopher Columbus* (New York: Corinth, 1961 [1847]), 196.

28   *"After we had rested"*: Michele de Cuneo, 1495 letter referring to January 20, 1594, quoted in Kirkpatrick Sale, *The Conquest of Paradise* (New York: Knopf, 1990), 143.

29   *I implore you*: The Requirement has been translated many times. This translation is from "500 Years of Indigenous and Popular Resistance Campaign" (np: Guatemala Committee for Peasant Unity, 1990).

30   *Diseases unknown to the Americas*: Alfred W. Crosby, *Ecological Imperatives: The Biological Expansion of Europe, 900–1900* (New York: Cambridge University Press, 1976), 71–93.

30   *So does the idea that "it's natural"*: bell hooks makes this point in "Columbus: Gone But Not Forgotten," Z, December 1992, 26.

31   *As early as 1915*: A.H. Lybyer, "The Ottoman Turks and the Oriental Trade," *English Historical Review* 30, no. 120 (October 1915), 577–88.

31   *Portugal did this to stop trade*: Lybyer.

32   *Columbus's purpose from the beginning*: Sale, 71–72.

32   *Many aspects of Columbus's life*: For the small fragments of knowledge about Columbus's background, see Lorenzo Camusso, *The Voyages of Columbus* (New York: Dorset, 1991), 9–10; Sale, 51–52.

36   *well-suited to Columbus's purpose*: Pietro Barozzi, "Navigation and Ships in the Age of Columbus," *Italian Journal* 5, no. 4 (1990), 38–41.

36   *"[t]hey were all getting on each other's nerves"*: Samuel Eliot Morison, *The Great Explorers* (New York: Oxford University Press, 1978), 397–98.

36   *Columbus himself wrote in his journal*: Cecil Jane, trans., *The Journal of Christopher Columbus* (New York: Bonanza, 1989), 171.

36 *textbooks have Columbus come to a tragic end*: Sale, 171, 185, 204–14, 362; John Hebert, ed., *1492: An Ongoing Voyage* (Washington, DC: Library of Congress, 1992), 100.

37 *"the most unpardonable offenses"*: Las Casas quoted in J.H. Elliot, *The Old World and the New* (New York: Cambridge University Press, 1970), 48.

37 *He wrote in his journal . . . "govern them as I pleased"*: The Log of Christopher Columbus's First Voyage to America in the Year 1492, as copied out in brief by Bartolomé de Las Cases (Hamden, CT: Linnet, 1989), unpaginated.

38 *On that first voyage, Columbus kidnapped*: Sale, 122.

38 *"For this he chose"*: Quoted in Michael Paiewonsky, *The Conquest of Eden, 1493–1515* (Chicago: Academy, 1991), 109. I have slightly modified the translation based on a translation in Juan Friede and Benjamin Keen, *Bartolomé de Las Casas in History* (De Kalb: Northern Illinois Press, 1971), 312.

38 *"In the name of the Holy Trinity"*: Christopher Columbus, 1496 letter, quoted in Eric Williams, *Documents of West Indian History* (Port-of-Spain, Trinidad: PNM, 1963), 1:57.

40 *Those who met their quotas . . . hands cut off*: Maria Norlander-Martinez, "Christopher Columbus: The Man, the Myth, and the Slave Trade," *Adventures of the Incredible Librarian*, April 1990, 17; Troy Floyd, *The Columbus Dynasty in the Caribbean* (Albuquerque, NM: University of New Mexico Press, 1973), 29.

40 *the* encomienda *system*: James Axtell, "Europeans, Indians, and the Age of Discovery in American History Textbooks," *American Historical Review* 92 (1987), 621–32; Sale, 156.

40 *"so as not to leave them"*: De Cordoba letter in Williams, 1:94.

41 *President Donald Trump said*: Holly Yan, "Trump's praise of Columbus omits dark history," CNN Politics, October 9, 2017, cnn.com/2017/10/09/politics/trump-obama-columbus-day/index.html.

42 *"the clash of cultures"*: Sale, 129.

42 *"Columbian exchange"*: Alfred W. Crosby Jr., *The Columbian Exchange: Biological and Cultural Consequences of 1492* (Westport, CT: Greenwood, 1972).

43 *Almost half the major crops . . . to England, France, Germany, and*

Russia: Crosby, *The Columbian Exchange*, 124–25 and chapter 5; William Langer, "American Foods and Europe's Population Growth, 1750–1850," *Journal of Social History* 8 (winter 1975), 51–66; Jack Weatherford, *Indian Givers* (New York: Fawcett, 1988), 65–71; "Seeds of Change" exhibit (Washington, DC: National Museum of Natural History, 1991).

Chapter 3: The Truth About the First Thanksgiving

45 *"How refreshing it would be"*: James Axtell, "Europeans, Indians, and the Age of Discovery in American History Textbooks," *American Historical Review* 92 (1987), 630.

46 *our first pilgrims*: Kathleen Teltsch, "Scholars and Descendants Uncover Hidden Legacy of Jews in Southwest," *New York Times*, November 11, 1990, A30; "Hidden Jews of the Southwest," *Groundrock* (Spring 1992).

46 *And somehow the English came to be seen*: James Axtell, "Europeans, Indians, and the Age of Discovery in American History Textbooks," *American Historical Review* 92 (1987), 640.

47 *In northern Europe and Asia*: William H. McNeill, "Disease in History," lecture at the University of Vermont, October 18, 1988.

47 *many diseases could not survive*: Alfred W. Crosby Jr., *The Columbian Exchange: Biological and Cultural Consequences of 1492* (Westport, CT: Greenwood, 1972), 34.

48 *He tried to get them to bathe*: Feenie Ziner, *Squanto* (Hamden, CT: Linnet Books, 1988), 141. It wasn't just the Pilgrims who didn't bathe. Queen Isabella of Spain boasted that she took only two baths in her life: one at birth and the other before her marriage, according to Jay Stuller, "Cleanliness," *Smithsonian* 21 (February 1991), 126–35.

49 *This disease and others*: William Langer, "The Black Death," *Scientific American*, February 1964; see also William H. McNeill, *Plagues and Peoples* (Garden City, NY: Doubleday, 1979), 166–85.

49 *Others suggest that it was*: Neal Salisbury, "Red Puritans: The 'Praying Indians' of Massachusetts Bay and John Eliot," in Bruce A.

Glasrud and Alan M. Smith, eds., *Race Relations in British North America, 1607–1783* (Chicago: Nelson-Hall, 1982), 44, and "Squanto: The Last of the Patuxets," in David Sweet and Gary Nash, eds., *Struggle and Survival in Colonial North America* (Berkeley and Los Angeles: University of California Press, 1981), 231–37; William Cronon, *Changes in the Land* (New York: Hill and Wang, 1983), 87.

50   *"miraculous"* . . . *"cleared our title"*: Quoted in Howard Simpson, *Invisible Armies: The Impact of Disease on American History* (Chapel Hill: University of North Carolina Press, 1975), 7.

50   *"God ended the controversy"*: John Winthrop to Simonds D'Ewes, July 21, 1643, *Publications of the Colonial Society of Massachusetts 1900–02*, 7 (December 1905) 71, at books.google.com/books.

50   *When the Spaniards marched in*: David Quammen, "Columbus and Submuloc," *Outside*, June 1990, 31–34; Crosby, *The Columbian Exchange*, 49; McNeill, *Plagues and Peoples*, 205–7.

51   *the isolated Yanomamo people*: James Brooke, "For an Amazon Indian Tribe, Civilization Brings Mostly Disease and Death," *New York Times*, December 24, 1989.

52   *By 1880, warfare and other pressures*: Peter Farb, *Man's Rise to Civilization* (New York: Avon, 1969), 294–95.

53   *"[I]t pleased God"*: William Bradford, *Of Plimouth Plantation*, rendered by Valerian Paget (New York: McBride, 1909), 258.

53   *Others think that the Pilgrims went*: The "on purpose" theory is supported by George F. Willison, *Saints and Strangers* (New York: Reynal and Hitchcock, 1945); Lincoln Kinnicutt, "The Settlement at Plymouth Contemplated Before 1620," *Publications of the American Historical Association* (1920), 211–21; and Neal Salisbury, *Manitou and Providence* (New York: Oxford University Press, 1982), 109, 270.

54   *The Pilgrims may have had . . . his guidebook instead*: Ziner, *Squanto*, 147; Kinnicutt, "The Settlement at Plymouth Contemplated Before 1620"; Almon W. Lauber, *Indian Slavery in Colonial Times Within the Present Limits of the United States* (Williamstown, MA: Corner House, 1970 [1913]), 156–59; Francis R. Stoddard, *The Truth about the Pilgrims* (New York: Society of Mayflower Descendants, 1952), 16.

57   *"We're the only idealistic nation"*: Woodrow Wilson, speech in Sioux Falls, September 8, 1919, in *Addresses of President Wilson* (Washington, DC: Government Printing Office, 1919), 86.

58   *"You know what I am?"* Donald Trump, quoted in Quint Forgey, "Trump: I'm a nationalist," *Politico*, October 22, 2018, https://www.politico.com/story/2018/10/22/trump-nationalist-926745.

58   *"fetch away the Treasure"*: Written by Robert Beverley in 1705, quoted in Wesley Frank Craven, *The Legend of the Founding Fathers* (Westport, CT: Greenwood, 1983 [1956]), 5–8.

60   *"In this bay wherein we live"*: Emmanuel Altham letter, quoted in Sydney V. James, ed., *Three Visitors to Early Plymouth* (Plymouth, MA: Plimoth Plantation, 1963), 29.

60   *the Pilgrims continued to rob graves*: Karen Ordahl Kupperman, *Settling with the Indians* (London: J.M. Dent, 1980), 125.

61   *"a special instrument"*: William Bradford, *Of Plymouth Plantation*, 99.

62   *"he was the sole member"*: Simpson, *Invisible Armies*, 6.

64   *embarrassing facts . . . until the 1870s*: Plimoth Plantation, "The American Thanksgiving Tradition, or How Thanksgiving Stole the Pilgrims" (Plymouth, MA: n.d., photocopy); Stoddard, *The Truth about the Pilgrims*, 13.

65   *"Today is a time of celebrating for you"*: Frank James, "Frank James' Speech" (New York Council on Interracial Books for Children *Bulletin* 10, no. 6, 1979), 13.

Chapter 4: Through Red Eyes

68   *"There is not one Indian"*: Rupert Costo, "There Is Not One Indian Who Has Not Come Home in Shame and Tears," in Miriam Wasserman, *Demystifying School* (New York: Praeger, 1974), 192–93.

71   *Various researchers have given estimates*: John N. Wilford, "New Mexico Cave Yields Clues to Early Man," *New York Times*, May 5, 1991; David Stannard, *American Holocaust* (New York: Oxford University Press, 1992), 10; Sharon Begley, "The First Americans," *Newsweek*, special issue, "When Worlds Collide," Fall/Winter 1991, 15–20; Andrew Murr, "Who Got Here First?" *News-*

week, November 15, 1999; Marc Stengel, "The Diffusionists Have Landed," *Atlantic Monthly*, January 1, 2000, 35–48; Steve Olson, "The Genetic Archaeology of Race," *Atlantic Monthly*, April 2001, 70–71, and "First Americans More Diverse Than Once Thought, Study Finds," *Washington Post*, July 31, 2001.

75 *"What is civilization?"*: Quoted in Rupert Costo and Jeanette Henry, *Textbooks and the American Indian* (San Francisco: Indian Historian Press, 1970).

78 *Ponce de León didn't go to Florida*: J. Leitch Wright Jr., *The Only Land They Knew* (New York: Free Press, 1981), 33, 130.

78 *The first Africans were brought*: Peter N. Carroll and David Noble, *The Free and the Unfree* (New York: Penguin, 1988), 57.

78 *In one year*: Almon W. Lauber, *Indian Slavery in Colonial Times Within the Present Limits of the United States* (Williamstown, MA: Corner House, 1970 [1913]), 106.

80 *In 1635, in the Dutch colony*: Ronald Sanders, *Lost Tribes and Promised Lands: The Origins of American Racism* (Boston: Little, Brown, 1978), 373–74.

80 *In 1794, when the zone of contact*: Helen H. Tanner, "The Glaize in 1792: A Composite Indian Community," *Ethnohistory* 25, no. 1 (Winter 1978), 15–39.

80 *Benjamin Franklin said*: Benjamin Franklin, quoted in Bruce Johnson, *Forgotten Founders: How the American Indian Helped Shape Democracy* (Cambridge, MA: Harvard Common Press, 1982), 92–93.

81 *"People who did run away"*: Karen Ordahl Kupperman, *Settling with the Indians* (London: J.M. Dent, 1980), 156.

82 *"All their government"*: Benjamin Franklin, quoted in Jose Barreiro, ed., *Indian Roots of American Democracy* (Ithaca, NY: Cornell University American Indian Program, 1988), 43.

82 *"six nations of ignorant savages"*: Benjamin Franklin, quoted in Bruce Johansen and Robert Maestas, *Wasichu: The Coming Indian Wars* (New York: Monthly Review Press, 1979), 35.

84 *Many of the regional dishes*: Jack Weatherford, *Indian Givers* (New York: Fawcett, 1988), ch. 6.

85 *"Does the textbook describe"*: Costo and Henry, *Textbooks and the American Indian*, 22.

86   *Textbooks should present*: Vine Deloria, an American Indian writer, does this in *God Is Red* (Golden, CO: North American Press, 1992 [1973]).

86   *"We took away their country"*: Quoted in Lee Clark Mitchell, *Witness to a Vanishing America* (Princeton, NJ: Princeton University Press, 1981), 200.

87   *In the real West*: Joe Feagin, *Racial and Ethnic Relations* (Englewood Cliffs, NJ: Prentice-Hall, 1982), 181; John D. Unruh, *The Plains Indians* (Urbana: University of Illinois Press, 1979).

88   *"It was a fearful sight"*: Quoted in Kupperman, *Settling with the Indians*, 185.

89   *By the end of the war*: Gary Nash, ed., *Red, White, and Black* (Englewood Cliffs, NJ: Prentice-Hall, 1974), 126.

93   *"A century of learning"*: Johansen, *Forgotten Founders*, 118.

94   *The Delaware Indians suggested this*: Francis Jennings, *Empire of Fortune* (New York: Norton, 1988), 479; see also Charles J. Kappler, *Indian Treaties 1778–1883* (New York: Interland, 1972 [1904]), 5.

94   *In the 1840s*: Ronald Satz, *American Indian Policy in the Jacksonian Era* (Lincoln: University of Nebraska Press, 1975), 216–18.

95   *"under penalty of death"*: S. Blancke and C.P.J. Slow Turtle, "The Teaching of the Past of the Native Peoples of North America in U.S. Schools," in Peter Stone and Robert MacKenzie, eds., *The Excluded Past* (London: Unwin Hyman, 1990), 123.

96   *In reality, the Cherokees*: Richard Drinnon, *Facing West* (Minneapolis: University of Minnesota Press, 1980), 85.

Chapter 5: Invisible Racism

99   *"The black-white rift"*: Ken Burns, "Mystic Chords of Memory," speech delivered at the University of Vermont, Burlington, September 12, 1991.

99   *"American obsession"*: Studs Terkel, *Race: How Blacks and Whites Think and Feel About the American Obsession* (New York: New Press, 1992).

100 *sweeping changes in the parties*: Thomas Byrne Edsall, *Chain Reac-*

tion (New York: Norton, 1991); "Willie Horton's Message," *New York Review of Books*, February 13, 1992, 7–11.

103 *"Our position is thoroughly identified"*: James W. Loewen and Edward H. Sebesta, *The Confederate and Neo-Confederate Reader* (Jackson: University Press of Mississippi, 2010), 114-16, 127.

105 *Massachusetts was the first colony . . . by the day or week*: Irving J. Sloan, *Blacks in America, 1492–1970* (Dobbs Ferry, NY: Oceana, 1971), 2; Howard Zinn, *The Politics of History* (Boston: Beacon Press, 1970), 67.

105 *Patrick Henry . . . "Would anyone believe"*: Richard R. Beeman, *Patrick Henry* (New York: McGraw-Hill, 1974), 182; Patrick Henry, quoted in J. Franklin Jameson, *The American Revolution Considered as a Social Movement* (Boston: Beacon Press, 1965), 23.

107 *"It is impossible for us to believe"*: Quoted in Felix Okoye, *The American Image of Africa: Myth and Reality* (Buffalo, NY: Black Academy Press, 1971), 37.

110 *First Seminole War*: Sloan, *Blacks in America*, 9; Daniel F. Littlefield Jr., *Africans and Creeks* (Westport, CT: Greenwood, 1979), 72–80.

110 *Second Seminole War*: J. Leitch Wright Jr., *The Only Land They Knew* (New York: Free Press, 1981), 277; William Loren Katz, *Teachers' Guide to American Negro History* (Chicago: Quadrangle, 1971), 34, 63; Scott Thybony, "Against All Odds, Black Seminole Won Their Freedom," *Smithsonian* 22, no. 5 (August 1991), 90–100; Littlefield, 85–90.

112 *"In my opinion this government of ours"*: Paul M. Angle, *Created Equal? The Complete Lincoln-Douglas Debates of 1858* (Chicago: University of Chicago Press, 1958), 22–23.

114 *"We tell the white men of Mississippi"*: James W. Loewen and Charles Sallis, eds., *Mississippi: Conflict and Change* (New York: Pantheon, 1980), 145–47.

118 *"the nadir of American race relations"*: Rayford W. Logan, *The Betrayal of the Negro* (New York: Macmillan, 1970 [1954]); Logan cites different dates for the nadir, but I would argue that mine are more accurate. See also Eric Foner, *Reconstruction* (New York: Harper & Row, 1988), 604.

118   *"These 'problems' seem to crop up"*: Frances FitzGerald, *America Revised* (New York: Vintage, 1980), 157.

120   *The Bronx Zoo, for example*: Irving Wallace, David Wallechinsky, and Amy Wallace, "Man in the Zoo," *Significa* (New York: Dutton, 1983), 26–27.

122   *One such riot took place*: Wallace, Wallechinsky, and Wallace, *Significa*, 60–61.

122   *Thousands of communities became "sundown towns"*: See James W. Loewen, *Sundown Towns: A Hidden Dimension of American Racism* (New York: New Press, 2005), especially ch. 3.

123   *Yet for decades the United States could not pass*: www.congress.gov/bill/115th-congress/senate-bill/3178/text?format=txt.

124   *in 2016 the median family income*: Jessica L. Semega, Kayla R. Fontenet, and Melissa A. Kollar, "Income and Poverty in the United States: 2016" (Washington, DC: U.S. Census Bureau, September 2017), census.gov/content/dam/Census/library/publications/2017/demo/P60-259.pdf.

124   *It's no surprise . . . less than white women's*: U.S. Department of Health and Human Services, "Health, United States, 2016" (Washington, DC: U.S. Government Printing Office, 2017), www.cdc.gov/nchs/data/hus/hus16.pdf#015.

Chapter 6: John Brown, Abraham Lincoln, and Invisible Idealism

127   *"You may dispose of me"*: John Brown, quoted by Henry David Thoreau in "A Plea for Captain John Brown," in Richard Scheidenhelm, ed., *The Response to John Brown* (Belmont, CA: Wadsworth, 1972), 58.

127   *"American political life"*: Frances FitzGerald, *America Revised* (New York: Vintage, 1980), 151.

131   *"the barns of all the jurors"*: Hannah Geffert and Jean Libby, "Regional Involvement in John Brown's Raid on Harpers Ferry," in T.P. McCarthy and J. Stauffer, eds., *Prophets of Protest* (New York: New Press, 2006), 173–175; Jean Libby, ed., *John Brown Mysteries*

(Missoula, MT: Pictorial Histories Publishing, 1999), 16–21, 25, 29–35.

132 *No reader of this account . . . they weren't*: Sara Robinson, *Kansas: Its Interior and Exterior Life*, ch. 16, kancoll.org/books/robinson/r _chapt16.htm; Marvin Stottlemirere, "John Brown: Madman or Martyr?" *Brown Quarterly* 3, no. 3 (Winter 2000); Louis A. DeCaro Jr., *John Brown—The Cost of Freedom* (New York: International, 2007), 41–42.

133 *"They are themselves mistaken"*: Stephen B. Oates, *To Purge This Land With Blood* (New York: Harper & Row, 1970), 329–34; Wise, "Message to the Virginia Legislature," reprinted in Scheidenhelm, ed., *The Response to John Brown*, 132–53. Of course, Governor Wise wanted to find Brown sane so that he could hang him, just as Brown's defenders argued that he was insane so that he would be spared. The best evidence of Brown's state of mind is his letters, statements, and interviews, which show no trace of insanity.

134 *"Now, if it is deemed necessary that I should forfeit my life"*: John Brown, "Last Words in Court," in Scheidenhelm, ed., *The Response to John Brown*, 36–37.

134 *"one of the greatest heroes"*: Benjamin Quarles, *The Black Abolitionists* (New York: Oxford University Press, 1969), 244.

135 *"While I cannot approve of all your acts"*: Letter quoted in William J. Schafer, ed., *The Truman Nelson Reader* (Amherst: University of Massachusetts Press, 1989), 250.

135 *Now whites generally came*: John Spencer Bassett, *A Short History of the United States* (New York: Macmillan, 1923), 502.

136 *"ten or twelve slaves . . . making me miserable"*: Richard Current, *The Lincoln Nobody Knows* (Westport, CT: Greenwood, 1980 [1958]), 216.

137 *"rock-solid antislavery beliefs"*: Richard H. Sewell, *A House Divided* (Baltimore: Johns Hopkins University Press, 1988), 74–75.

137 *"If slavery isn't wrong"*: Abraham Lincoln, letter to Albert Hodges, April 4, 1864; full text in Herbert Aptheker, *And Why Not Every Man?* (New York: International, 1961), 249.

139 *It even hurt him politically*: V.J. Voegeli, *Free but Not Equal* (Chicago: University of Chicago Press, 1967), 62–63, 128–50.

142 *"And although he may be poor"*: Lyrics quoted in James M. McPherson, *Battle Cry of Freedom* (New York: Oxford University Press, 1988), vi.

142 *One Union captain wrote to his wife*: Quoted in James M. McPherson, "Wartime," *New York Review of Books*, March 12, 1990, 33.

143 *"The change of opinion"*: Quoted by McPherson, *Battle Cry of Freedom*, 688 (his ellipsis).

143 *"the protection of slavery"*: Paul Escott, *After Secession* (Baton Rouge: Louisiana State University Press, 1978), 254.

144 *Throughout the war . . . prevent slave uprisings*: Carleton Beals, *War Within a War* (Philadelphia: Chilton, 1965), 12, 142.

147 *"If slaves will make good soldiers"*: Howell Cobb, quoted in Robert C. Kennedy, "Impetuous Charge of the First Colored Rebel Regiment," *New York Times* "On This Day," November 5, 2001, archive. nytimes.com/www.nytimes.com/learning/general/onthisday/harp/1105.html.

147 *Meanwhile, almost two-thirds of the Confederate army*: Barrie Stavis, *John Brown: The Sword and the Word* (New York: A.S. Barnes, 1970), 1012; see also McPherson, *Battle Cry of Freedom*, 832–38; Joseph T. Glatthaar, *The March to the Sea and Beyond* (Baton Rouge: Louisiana State University Press, 1995). Until the last year of the war, Union desertion rates were almost as high as Confederate rates, but Union deserters almost never joined the Confederate army.

148 *"shot but none killed"*: Edmonia Highgate, quoted in Robert Moore, *Reconstruction: The Promise and Betrayal of Democracy* (New York: CIBC, 1983), 17.

149 *One of them was a Mississippi planter . . . newspaper called* Equal Rights: William C. Harris, "A Reconsideration of the Mississippi Scalawag," *Journal of Mississippi History* 37, no. 1 (February 1970), 11013.

149 *The U.S. Congress had . . . from wealthy families*: Harris, "A Reconsideration of the Mississippi Scalawag," 3–42; C. Vann Woodward, "Unfinished Business," *New York Review of Books*, May 12, 1988.

Chapter 7: The Land of Opportunity

153 *One easy way . . . less than 21%*: Andrea Brandolini, "On the Iden-
tification of the 'Middle Class,'" June 2010, fig. 4; DQYDJ, "United
States Household Income Brackets and Percentiles in 2017," dqydj
.com/united-states-household-income-brackets-percentiles.

154 *On average death . . . health care for those with money*: The difference
is dramatically documented in the film *Health Care: Your Money or
Your Life* (New York: Downtown Community TV Center, c. 1977). It
compares two publicly funded hospitals in New York City, one caring
mostly for poor people, the other for people with more money.

155 *A historian named Edward Pessen*: Edward Pessen, *The Log Cabin
Myth* (New Haven: Yale University Press, 1984).

155 *Most men and boys*: August Hollingshead and Frederick C. Redlich,
Social Class and Mental Illness (New York: Wiley, 1958), 6.

156 *"the hidden injuries of class"*: Richard Sennett and Jonathan Cobb,
The Hidden Injuries of Class (New York: Knopf, 1972).

157 *One 2018 study*: "Income inequality," Organisation for Economic
Co-operation and Development, 2018, data.oecd.org/inequality/
income-inequality.htm.

158 *In 2016, according to the Federal Reserve Bank*: "Changes in U.S.
Family Finances from 2013 to 2016: Evidence from the Survey of
Consumer Finances," *Federal Reserve Bulletin*, vol. 103, no. 3, Sep-
tember 2017, federalreserve.gov/publications/files/scf17.pdf.

158 *But the top one-fifth*: "Shares of household income of quintiles
in the United States from 1970 to 2016," Statista, statista.com/
statistics/203247/shares-of-household-income-of-quintiles-in-the-
us/.

158 *In 1967 . . . the average worker's pay*: "Index," *Harper's*, May 1990,
19; Jeanne Sahadi, "CEO Pay: Sky High Gets Even Higher,"
CNNMoney.com, August 30, 2005.

158 *In 2017, the richest 1% . . . of the nation's wealth*: Christopher Ingra-
ham, "The richest 1 percent now owns more of the country's wealth
than at any time in the past 50 years," *Washington Post*, December
6, 2017, washingtonpost.com/news/wonk/wp/2017/12/06/.

Chapter 8: Keeping an Eye on the Government

160 *"What did you learn in school"*: Lyrics from Tom Paxton's "That's What I Learned in School," Cherry Lane Music Co., Inc., all rights reserved, used by permission, copyright 1962, 1990.

162 *"We have about 50%"*: George Kennan, quoted in Sheila D. Collins, "From the Bottom Up and the Outside In," *CALC Report* 15, no. 3 (March 1990), 9–10.

164 *The same could be said*: Interviews with high-level managers of multinational corporations in Larry Adelman's video *Controlling Interest: The World of Multinational Corporations* (San Francisco: California Newsreel, 1978) show their influence, particularly over U.S. policy in Chile.

165 *"I helped make Mexico safe"*: Gen. Smedley D. Butler, quoted in a *New York Times* interview, August 21, 1931, reprinted in Joseph R. Conlin, ed., *The Morrow Book of Questions in American History* (New York: Morrow, 1984), 58.

166 *according to historian Barry Weisberg*: Barry Weisberg, *Beyond Repair* (Boston: Beacon Press, 1971), 79.

168 *According to testimony given to the U.S. Senate*: Pierre Salinger, "Gaps in the Cuban Missile Crisis Story," *New York Times*, February 5, 1989; Lewis H. Lapham, *America's Century Series Transcript* (San Francisco: KQED, 1989), 51; Charles Ameringer, *U.S. Foreign Intelligence* (Lexington, MA: D.C. Heath, 1990), 285–95; Rhodri Jeffrey-Jones, *The CIA and American Democracy* (New Haven: Yale University Press, 1989), 131–40.

170 *During the 1950s, at least 31 U.S. flights*: Thomas W. Lippman, "138 Reported Missing in U.S. Spy Flights," *Washington Post*, March 5, 1993; Thomas Powers, "Notes from Underground," *New York Review of Books*, June 21, 2001, 51.

172 *In its early years*: Kenneth O'Reilly, *Racial Matters* (New York: Free Press, 1989), 9, 12–13, 17, 96-99; Ameringer, *U.S. Foreign Policy*, 109.

172 *In 1963 he launched a campaign . . . his wife to divorce him*: O'Reilly, *Racial Matters*, 43, 126, 144, 355; David J. Garrow, *The FBI and*

Martin Luther King Jr. (New York: Penguin, 1981), 125–26, 161–64; Taylor Branch, *Parting the Waters* (New York: Simon & Schuster, 1988), 861; Ameringer, *U.S. Foreign Intelligence*, 322–23; Frank J. Donner, *The Age of Surveillance* (New York: Knopf, 1980), 214–19; Athan Theoharis and John Stuart Cox, *The Boss* (Philadelphia: Temple University Press, 354–57.

172   *It also refused to share*: Branch, *Parting the Waters*, 692.

173   *a bowling alley in Orangeburg . . . defend themselves in court*: O'Reilly, *Racial Matters*, 256; Arlie Schardt, "Civil Rights: Too Much, Too Late," in Pat Watters and Stephen Gillers, *Investigating the FBI* (New York: Ballantine, 1973), 167–79.

173   *"out-of-state Negro speakers"*: O'Reilly, *Racial Matters*, 336–37; Donner, *The Age of Surveillance*, 29–20.

176   *"We live in the greatest country"*: Critique by James F. Delong (Hoover, AL: 1896, typescript distributed by Mel Gabler's Educational Research Analysts, 1993).

Chapter 9: Seeing No Evil in Vietnam

178   *"Without censorship"*: General William C. Westmoreland, quoted at Brainy Quote, brainyquote.com, May 2007; Antiwar, antiwar.com/quotes.php, May 2007; and elsewhere.

178   *In fact, people who graduated from high school*: Students' ignorance about Vietnam was no accident. According to historian Michael Kammen, in *Mystic Chords of Memory* (New York: Knopf, 1991), 661–62, President Gerald Ford wanted us to forget Vietnam. President Ronald Reagan slashed the National Archives budget and kept documents "secret" longer to interfere with our knowledge of recent history.

182   *"It does deprive the enemy"*: General William C. Westmoreland, quoted in Murray Kempton, "Heart of Darkness," *New York Review of Books*, November 24, 1988, 26.

184   *"not isolated incidents but crimes"*: John Kerry, "Winter Soldier Investigation," testimony to U.S. Senate Foreign Relations Committee, April 1971, reprinted in William Appleman Williams et al.,

eds., *America in Vietnam* (New York: Norton, 1989), 295.; see also "Declassified Papers Show U.S. Atrocities in Vietnam Went Far Beyond My Lai," *Los Angeles Times*, August 6, 2006, at History News Network,hnn.us/roundup/entries/28956.html.

190 *By 1986, at least 70% of Americans*: Gallup poll, November 1986; Roper poll, August 1984.

Chapter 10: The Disappearance of the Recent Past

192 *"When information which properly belongs"*: Presidential proclamation in 1972 to strengthen the Freedom of Information Act, quoted in Tim Weiner, "The Cold War Freezer Keeps Historians Out," *New York Times*, May 23, 1993.

192 *Some eastern and central African societies*: John Mbiti, *African Religions and Philosophy* (Oxford, UK: Heinemann, 1990).

199 *"Americans are asking"*: George W. Bush, Address to Joint Session of Congress, September 20, 2001, whitehouse.gov/news/releases /2001/09/20010920-8.html.

201 *"The soldiers, spies, academics"*: James Fallows's articles are summarized in his *Blind into Baghdad* (New York: Random House Vintage, 2006).

201 *"Bin Laden has been precise"*: Michael Scheuer, quoted in Jason Bourke, "Will the Real al-Qaida Please Stand Up," *The Guardian*, March 11, 2006, guardian.co.uk/review/story/0,,1726185.00html.

201 *"Muslims do not 'hate our freedom'"*: Pentagon report, November 2004, quoted in Thom Shanker, "U.S. Failing to Persuade Muslims, Panel Says," *International Herald Tribune*, November 25, 2004.

202 *More than a month before the attacks*: Gerald Posner, *Why America Slept* (New York: Random House, 2003), 121, 152, 157, 169; Anthony Lappé and Stephen Marshall, *True Lies* (New York: Penguin Plume, 2004), 52–53.

Chapter 11: History and the Future

208 *"Americans see history as a straight line"*: Frances FitzGerald, *Fire in the Lake* (Boston: Atlantic–Little, Brown, 1972), 8.

208 *Thomas Jefferson wrote of an imaginary journey*: Thomas Jefferson, quoted in Robert Nisbet, *The Idea of Progress* (New York: Basic Books, 1980), 198.

209 *We boasted about*: According to the Advertising Council's citizenship manual, *Good Citizen*, quoted in Stuart Little, "The Freedom Train," *American Studies* (34)1, Spring 1993.(Bloomington: Indiana University, c. 1990, typescript), 11.

210 *In 1850, average national income . . . twenty to sixty times*: Edward H. Carr, *What Is History?* (New York: Random House, 1961), 116; L. Stavrianos, *Global Rift* (New York: Morrow, 1981), 38; see also Cliff DuRand, "Mexico-U.S. Migration: We Fly, They Walk," talk at Morgan State University, November 16, 2005, worldproutassem bly.org/archives/2006/01/mexicous_migrat.html; Giovanni Arrighi, "The African Crisis," *New Left Review* 15, May 2002, newleftrev iew.org/?page=article&view=2387.

211 *"Future historians will probably record"*: Gabriel Almond et al., eds., *Progress and Its Discontents* (Berkeley and Los Angeles: University of California Press, 1982), xi.

211 *In 2011, only 44% . . . fallen to 30*: "Emerging and Developing Economies Much More Optimistic than Rich Countries about the Future," Pew Research Center, Global Attitudes & Trends, October 9, 2014, pewglobal.org/2014/10/09/.

212 *People's general happiness*: General Social Survey, NORC, 2015, norc.org/PDFs/GSS%20Reports/GSS_PsyWellBeing15_final_for matted.pdf.

214 *the catch had fallen to just 166,000 bushels*: B.D. Ayers Jr., "Hard Times for Chesapeake's Oyster Harvest," *New York Times*, October 15, 1993; David E. Pitt, "U.N. Talks Combat Threat to Fishery," *New York Times*, July 25, 1993; Pitt, "Despite Gaps, Data Leave Little Doubt that Fish Are in Peril," *New York Times*, August 3, 1993.

214 *In 2006* Science *magazine reported*: Elizabeth Weise, "90% of the

Ocean's Edible Species May Be Gone by 2048, Study Finds," *USA Today*, November 3, 2006.

215 *"Scientists are haunted"*: Joel Achenbach, "The Tempest," *Washington Post Magazine*, May 28, 2006, 24.

217 *In 2018, factories in China were still making*: Chris Buckley and Henry Fountain, "In a High-Stakes Environmental Whodunit, Many Clues Point to China," *New York Times*, June 24, 2018, nytimes.com/2018/06/24/world/asia/china-ozone-cfc.html.

220 *"these islands had been"*: Spanish letter quoted in Kirkpatrick Sale, *The Conquest of Paradise* (New York: Knopf, 1990), 165.

222 *By 1992, only half of all women*: "Harper's Index," *Harper's*, February 1993, 15, citing Ross Labs.

224 *A 1993 survey found that*: Ruth Bond, "In the Ozone, a Child Shall Lead Them," *New York Times*, January 10, 1993.

224 *A survey of high-school seniors in 1999*: National Association of Secretaries of State New Millennium Survey, 1999,stateofthevote.org/New%20Mill%20Survey%20Update.pdf.

224 *By 2014, about half*: Pew Research Center, "Beyond Red vs. Blue: The Political Typology," Section 2: Views of the Nation, the Constitution and Government, June 26, 2014, www.people-press .org/2014/06/26/.

Chapter 12: Does This Way of Teaching History Work?

225 *"When you're publishing a book"*: Quoted in Joan DelFattore, *What Johnny Shouldn't Read* (New Haven: Yale University Press, 1992), 120.

226 *In 1925 the American Legion claimed*: Quoted in Bessie L. Pierce, *Public Opinion and the Teaching of History in the United States* (New York: Knopf, 1926), 329–30.

226 *In contrast, Shirley Engle and Anna Ochoa*: Shirley Engle and Anna Ochoa, "A Curriculum for Democratic Citizenship," *Social Education* (November 1986), 515.

226 *Historian Marc Ferro argued*: Marc Ferro, *The Use and Abuse of History* (Boston: Routledge and Kegan Paul, 1981), 225.

228 *"books that contain dangerous ideas"*: Gallup poll, October 1987, reported in *Stamford* [CT] *Advocate*, December 26, 1987, 1.

228 *He meant that those in power*: I do not mean to imply that "the upper class" controls our textbooks. See James W. Loewen, "What Do You Do When a Review Is Dishonest?" History News Network, May 25, 2015; see historynewsnetwork.org/blog/153629 for a fuller discussion of this complex point.

229 *"It is absolutely the standard practice"*: Judith Conaway, interview, July 2006.

229 *"They pick up things pretty quickly"*: Textbook editor, interview, July 2006.

230 *"[T]extbooks mirror our society"*: John Williamson, quoted in J.Y. Cole and T.G. Sticht, eds., *The Textbook in American Society* (Washington, DC: Library of Congress, 1981), 39.

231 *Unfortunately, that legend was made up*: "Cherry Tree Myth," Washington Library, Center for Digital History, mountvernon.org/library/digitalhistory/digital-encyclopedia/article/cherry-tree-myth.

231 *"When I first learned that Washington and Jefferson had slaves"*: Mark Lloyd, interview, 1991.

233 *When two-thirds of seventeen-year-old Americans*: Diane Ravitch and Chester E. Finn, *What Do Our 17-Year-Olds Know?* (New York: Harper & Row, 1987), 49.

234 *The movie* A Class Divided: PBS *Frontline* video, Washington, DC, 1985.

Afterword: The Future Lies Ahead—and What to Do About Them

237 *"Once you have learned"*: Neil Postman and Charles Weingartner, *Teaching as a Subversive Activity* (New York: Delacorte, 1969), 23.

245 *Thomas Jefferson urged the teaching of political history*: Quoted in Lewis H. Lapham, "Notebook," *Harper's*, July 1991, 12.

Index

Page numbers in italics indicate illustrations.

JAMES W. LOEWEN is the bestselling and award-winning author of *Lies My Teacher Told Me, Lies Across America, Lies My Teacher Told Me About Christopher Columbus*, and *Sundown Towns* (all from The New Press). He also wrote *Teaching What Really Happened* and *The Mississippi Chinese: Between Black and White* and edited *The Confederate and Neo-Confederate Reader*. He has won the American Book Award, the Oliver Cromwell Cox Award for Distinguished Anti-Racist Scholarship, the Spirit of America Award from the National Council for the Social Studies, and the Gustavus Myers Outstanding Book Award. Loewen is professor emeritus of sociology at the University of Vermont and lives in Washington, DC.

REBECCA STEFOFF has devoted her career to writing nonfiction books for young readers. She has adapted works including Howard Zinn's *A People's History of the United States*, Jared Diamond's *The Third Chimpanzee*, and Charles C. Mann's bestselling *1491*. She lives in Portland, Oregon.

Publishing in the Public Interest

Thank you for reading this book published by The New Press. The New Press is a nonprofit, public interest publisher. New Press books and authors play a crucial role in sparking conversations about the key political and social issues of our day.

We hope you enjoyed this book and that you will stay in touch with The New Press. Here are a few ways to stay up to date with our books, events, and the issues we cover:

* Sign up at www.thenewpress.com/subscribe to receive updates on New Press authors and issues and to be notified about local events

* Like us on Facebook: www.facebook.com/newpressbooks

* Follow us on Twitter: www.twitter.com/thenewpress

Please consider buying New Press books for yourself; for friends and family; or to donate to schools, libraries, community centers, prison libraries, and other organizations involved with the issues our authors write about.

The New Press is a 501(c)(3) nonprofit organization. You can also support our work with a tax-deductible gift by visiting www.thenewpress.com/donate.